Praise for *What About Me?*

"Dr. Jane Greer's book *What About Me?* is a must-read. From page one it showed me how to view relationships in a different light. This book is both insightful and empowering. I learned that what is important is not who is right or wrong, but how to compromise and become a winning team. Very inspiring!"

—Vanessa Williams, award-winning actress/singer

"*What About Me?* unabashedly digs deeply into the origins of conflict in relationships and paves the way for resolution, healing, and happiness. This is a book that will serve all of us well, not just in our relationships with others, but in our understanding of our complex selves."

—David Perlmutter, MD, author of *Power Up Your Brain: The Neuroscience of Enlightenment*

"I wish I had read Dr. Jane Greer's new book *What About Me?* before my first 6,000 disastrous relationships. Listen, getting from "me" to "we" is hard enough for normal people, let alone self-centered talk show hosts like me. She has also counseled me in person, and she is always annoyingly accurate. You need this book, trust me!"

—Stephanie Miller, nationally syndicated radio host and television pundit

"Finally, a simply put yet deeply resonating guide to help us eliminate toxic messages that feed into our relationships! Keep *What About Me?* next to your bedside and get what you need, immediately!"

—Emme, supermodel

"Before you set forth to solve the riddle of married life, you and your partner should read this book. It offers a perspective on the deepest kinds of self-centered problems and situations that can ruin a union. It will give each of you an ongoing frame of reference to help you know yourself better and to understand the inevitable challenges each of you will face."

—Bill Boggs, TV host and self-empowerment speaker

"Cutting through the veil of selfishness with a step-by-step velvet glove approach, Dr. Jane's book truly leads the way to relationship happiness."

—Linda Mackenzie, founder, HealthyLife.net
Radio Network

What About Me?

What About Me?

Stop Selfishness from Ruining Your Relationship

DR. JANE GREER

sourcebooks
casablanca

Published by Sourcebooks Casablanca, an imprint of Sourcebooks, Inc.
P.O. Box 4410, Naperville, Illinois 60567-4410
(630) 961-3900
Fax: (630) 961-2168
www.sourcebooks.com

Library of Congress Cataloging-in-Publication Data

Greer, Jane.
What about me? : stop selfishness from ruining your relationship / by Jane Greer.
p. cm.
1. Interpersonal relations. 2. Man-woman relationships. 3. Couples. 4. Selfishness.
I. Title.
HM1106.G744 2010
646.7'8--dc22
2010027319

Printed and bound in the United States of America.
VP 10 9 8 7 6 5 4 3 2 1

To my husband Marc
for that defining Sunday
and for all the days of sharing your love

Contents

Acknowledgments

THE ESSENCE OF THIS BOOK IS ABOUT SHARING. I WANT TO share my gratitude and profound thanks with the people who, because of their willingness to give an unlimited amount of their energy and time, made this book possible.

Here's the short list:

Heidi Krupp-Lisiten, for your expertise and certainty that started everything and connected me to exactly the right person who could help me craft a book.

Lisa Berkowitz, you have been and remain amazing. This book happened only because of your creative vision, remarkable ability, savvy wisdom, and dedication and unwavering belief in and support of me from start to finish.

Colleen Oakley, it was truly your "dream team" tenacity and steadfast perseverance that launched this project and got it off the ground.

Elizabeth LaBan, from the very first sentence, your stroke of genius brought this book to life. Collaborating with you has been an exhilarating cosmic experience and an absolute joy. Thank you for your talent, your "words and music," and for always going the distance.

Uwe Stender, for finding the right "house" to be the perfect home.

Shana Drehs, for giving me your hands-on support and clarity throughout the book, along with your sharp editorial smarts.

Maria Papapetros, for your astounding "title" vision and our ongoing unique connection.

Joanie Lienwoll, for streamlining my life, running the show, and giving me breathing room. You are a real gift.

I want to thank my patients for sharing their trust and letting me help. And I want to thank my incredible family, "personal manager" Carol April, and equally incredible "family" of friends who always see me through—you know who you are.

Special thanks to Kathy Pomerantz Feldman, for always being there in all the moments big and small, and to Dr. Josie Palleja, for all the years of love and friendship.

Author's Note

As a psychotherapist, I consider it my first priority to safeguard the confidentiality of my patients and interview subjects. In the interest of protecting their privacy, I have changed the names of all persons mentioned in this book, except for those in my family. I have also altered the details of people's lives—their professions, backgrounds, and other potentially identifying circumstances.

Introduction

LYDIA AND JAKE HAVEN'T HAD SEX IN TWO MONTHS. LYDIA can't figure out how they reached this point. Jake, on the other hand, blames it on the makeup mirror in their bathroom. About six months ago, he told Lydia to please push the extending arm of the mirror back against the wall when she's done with it, because he was constantly bumping into it as he got ready for bed. But she never remembers! So every night Jake hits his head, sometimes hard, realizes she forgot—or that she chose not to do this simple thing—and feels immediately angry. By the time he gets into bed, he's seething, and the last thing he wants to do is be nice to his wife. He doesn't turn to her the way he used to do, with his head on his pillow, and take her hand. He doesn't kiss her or gently tickle her like he has done for most of their marriage. He stares straight ahead, or grabs his book, and the road to sex is blocked.

For Lydia and Jake it is the makeup mirror, but your complaint could be anything—the toilet seat that is never put down, the kitchen drawer that is always left open, your partner's shoes that you constantly trip over. It is that annoying thing in your relationship that you keep banging into, the thing that makes you wonder why your partner can't make this one change for you. It's a Selfish Hot Spot, an action that drives you crazy and leads to a Selfish Standoff, an impasse in your relationship you just can't seem to get past.

Everyone has needs and desires. That is indisputable. Put two people together, and the likelihood that their needs will correspond exactly is slim to none. Sure, sometimes people want the same things: to get married, to have children, to keep the house thermostat at an even 68 degrees summer or winter. But what happens when, even if in theory people want the same things, they don't want them at the same time? Or what about when people don't want the same things at all? He likes a cold house, but she wants it to be warm. She wants to get engaged, but he wants to wait and see how it goes. Jake wants that mirror against the wall every time Lydia leaves the bathroom. But Lydia, who isn't tall enough to be bothered by the mirror, can't see what the big deal is. She tries to remember, but if she doesn't, she wonders why he can't just turn it around himself.

Is one person's need more important than another's? If Jake gets his way, isn't he being selfish? If Lydia can't do this for Jake, isn't she thinking only of herself?

Welcome to the Selfish Game. You start out having fun with your partner, both wanting to share. However, somewhere along the way the game becomes competitive without your even realizing it, because if you are one of two people with different needs, a clash is inevitable. You end up pitting your needs against each other instead of being able to find a compromise, so that in the end there is either a winner or a loser. The minute that you have any differences in style, taste, preference, or personality that require a sacrifice from either you or your partner, it is going to raise the question of whether one of you is being selfish. And the game is afoot.

In every relationship you have basic needs that constantly simmer below the details of life. You're looking to feel loved, desired, valued, accepted, safe, and secure. You want to please your partner and be pleased by them. You want attention, and you want your thoughts, ideas, and feelings to be validated. You want to see your best reflected in your loved one's eyes—the admiration, attraction, desire, and respect that you hope your partner has for you.

But that is hard to sustain. As the relationship grows, it's inevitable that selfish behavior will creep in on both sides as you become more comfortable with your partner and worry less about pleasing them. You start out picture-perfect but grow ugly to each other over time, because you are seeing your worst reflected back at you. And it is so surprising, because you began your relationship, as everyone does, seeing that adoring look of love. That's what I call the mirror of romance. It's one of the main things that brought you and your partner together in the first place. And you expect it to always be that way. So often, though, the mirror of romance fades with time, transforming into a judgment mirror that reflects only the bad you.

Please, join me in my office. Take a seat on the cream couch over there. Don't mind my dog, Totopuff, a.k.a. Puffy. He won't bother you. And listen with me to the toll selfishness takes on relationships as people deal with the ins and outs of daily living and how they are conquering the Selfish Game, one Hot Spot at a time.

Max was in my office recently. He didn't want to work on his marriage. Why bother, he asked. Shouldn't it just fall into place? I replied, okay, if you don't want to work on how to get along better in a positive way with your wife, then let's work on how you're going to end your marriage. That's a ton of work in itself by the time you figure out the finances, living situations, emotions. Then, after you're finally through the turmoil of the divorce, you'll be single again and have to take the next step of meeting someone else. And then, once you're finally in another relationship, you're going to have to work on that. So, I told Max, pick your poison. Do you want to do the work now or do it later? He laughed and said okay, he got it. He was ready to work on his marriage.

Nobody gets a pass on doing the work. If you want to have the other person in your life, and it is worth it to you to make the effort, then you won't feel like your life is being interrupted by that person and that it is a bother to stop what you are doing to make time for your partner.

I believe that if people have the proper knowledge and skills, they will better be able to reconcile their differences. But more often than not, they're not prepared, so they end up in scenarios in which the emotional and sexual issues are played out, often leading to those Selfish Standoffs I mentioned earlier, as well as

Sexual Showdowns. This book will equip you with the tools you need to see beyond what you see as selfish requests and to learn to understand all the differences, fears, and preferences that come between people. By understanding them, you'll see these are not the only measures that determine whether you are loved by the person you are with. You will get a sense of what is causing the problems in your relationship and how you are eventually going to resolve them. And you will know better how to communicate with your partner and consider each other's needs.

This power struggle between what *I* want versus what *you* want has existed between all couples since the beginning of time, but it is more pronounced in the twenty-first-century entitlement explosion. Self-centeredness is acceptable and encouraged and has reached epidemic proportions.

Everyone feels that they deserve to get exactly what they want when they want it, and it's wreaking havoc with our relationships. Couples are constantly squabbling, jockeying for position, and searching for ways to get their needs met—either with no regard for their partner's feelings, with great guilt over their perceived selfishness, or something in-between. On the other side, people are trying to make sense of living with partners who appear to be all about themselves: self-absorbed, self-centered, self-indulgent, narcissistic.

And this is a new brand of selfishness, because thanks to advancements in technology, there is a pervasive overtone in society that supports the me mentality. Everything is instant, new and improved, satisfaction guaranteed. When something is broken, we'd rather replace it than fix it, and that attitude has bled over to relationships. The world is in the palm of your hand, and almost everything you desire can be a click away.

People enjoy being connected to everyone, but that is sometimes at the expense of being disconnected from someone who really matters. Thoughtlessness and discourteousness are now the norm instead of the exception. Accepting a phone call during dinner used to be considered rude; now it's the rule. People think they are sharing more by tweeting, texting, and blogging about their personal lives, but they're actually warping the foundation of trust. If you share everything with everybody on an open blog, then how do you create the intimacy that sharing personal information with just one person brings? Facebook and LinkedIn have taken the place of quality time that you used to spend with your loved one. Work is now a twenty-four-hour-a-day gig where you are answering emails over romantic dinners on your iPhone or BlackBerry.

If you manage your time wisely, these independent activities can be part of a healthy, full life and relationship. But too often, people aren't budgeting their time effectively. They're prioritizing these distractions above all else, including their relationship. Never before has the lament "You're not listening to me" rung so true. In fact, people are listening to and paying attention to everyone and everything except their partner and their relationship. Porn is a click away, old flames are waiting on Facebook, and if that isn't enough, finding a new lover is as simple as logging on to MarriedMatch.com. Or if you've already got that part-time lover, there are websites like Alibi.com to help you keep the ruse going. Our system has evolved and become fine-tuned toward encouraging and enhancing personal gratification and double-life activity more than ever before.

But the gimme generation expects nothing less than that. Baby boomers, making up for what they didn't have, indulged their children's every whim. They are raising their kids as if they are the center of the universe, creating an entire generation that expects to get what they want when they want it, be it a new car, a five-hundred-dollar purse, or a partner at their beck and call. In the popular 2009 book *The Narcissism Epidemic: Living in the Age of Entitlement,* authors Rose M. Twenge and W. Keith Campbell eloquently sum up the state of the selfishness epidemic in America: "For the past several years, Americans have been buying McMansions and expensive cars on credit they can't afford. Although these seem like a random collection of current trends, all are rooted in a single underlying shift in American culture: the relentless rise of narcissism, a very positive and inflated view of self."

This new brand of selfishness is compounded by the fact that people today have more to do and less time to do it in than ever before. Your kids, your boss, your parents, your friends all want a piece of you. Quality time is no longer kicking back on a porch swing with a glass of lemonade. It's half listening to your husband while tweeting on your iPhone, sending a call from your boss to voice mail, with your kid's video game blaring in the background. So when it comes down to giving time to your partner, it can feel like a loss of your personal needs rather than an expression of love.

If you're giving the little bit of time you have left over to your partner, how can you take care of and give time to yourself? Doing anything for somebody you care about feels like taking it away from you, like you're relinquishing your own space and needs.

This tug-of-war is increasingly apparent not only in recent divorce statistics—one in two American marriages ends in divorce—but also in the rising numbers of cohabitation. Between 1990 and 2000 the number of unmarried couples living together rose by 72 percent, according to the U.S. Census. People are hedging their bets for fear of getting married. Yet the desire to be married continues to prevail. Even though the United States has the highest divorce rate in the Western world, Americans also have the highest marriage rate (90 percent of us will wed in our lifetimes, according to the 2000 World Values Survey), and only 10 percent of Americans believe marriage is "an outdated institution" (compared with 36 percent of the French). One can only conclude that Americans want to be married, and they want to make it work; they just need the road map to get there.

In my more than twenty years as a marriage and sex therapist, as well as a psychotherapist, author, media consultant, radio host, and adjunct professor, I've seen hundreds of couples grapple with these issues in my office on a weekly basis and also in the larger setting of television studios and seminars. I have a front-row seat to what is going on behind closed doors, and I know that arguing and fighting between couples is at an all-time high—it's what's leading not only to divorce but to so much infidelity. In today's world, options are everywhere. It takes a great effort to stay faithful, continue to honor your commitment, and do the work it takes to keep your relationship strong. While statistics are harder to come by for adultery due to the obvious secrecy surrounding the issue, it's estimated that up to half of all married partners cheat on their spouses. Like a growing autoimmune disease, the recent rise in marital combat, infidelity, and divorce are all symptomatic of the selfishness epidemic.

This sense of entitlement and expectation created by these changes in our culture has resulted in partners being pitted against each other more than ever. Instead of being a team and sharing the burden of outside pressures, partners are buckling under the weight of their own needs and how to meet them. There is a push and pull of what *I* want versus what *you* want and my needs versus your needs, resulting in endless stalemates and standoffs.

Call it what you like, but relationships have been whittled down to a recurring theme: me versus we. It should be that relationships are about creating a *we* identity, without losing or sacrificing your *me* identity. Unfortunately, sharing and communication, the cornerstones of strong relationships and major ingredients of the *we* identity, have been eroded. In order to restore a balance, people need clarity about themselves: how selfish they are, what's reasonable to expect of themselves and their partner, and most important, what's realistic.

This is not just a book for those of you in relationships. It's also a book for singles, because so many single people are scared of getting in a relationship for these very reasons: you don't want to give up your identity or your need for space. "I need my space" is a universal way of saying "I need to do my own thing and at this time am unwilling to make the time for you," which, of course, is often translated by a partner or potential partner to mean "I am being selfish." I will help you understand why you feel this way and that it's possible to have a relationship that doesn't strip you of your identity.

In part 1 of *What About Me?* I will look at the role you play in your relationship and how that leads to different expectations you have of your partner. I will also identify some of the most common Selfish Hot Spots and sexual issues that can bring you to your knees. In part 2 I will delve deeper into the issues you and your partner clash over and offer you tools to talk in a more loving way. You will also learn the steps you can take toward healthy SelfNess and the importance of standing up for your needs. You will learn how to better manage your guilt, resentment, disappointment, and anger so that you can compromise and share in order to become caring partners. Most important, you will figure out how to work as a team to make your relationship strong. I believe that you will work harder and be better able to salvage your relationship if you know how to do these things. You will be better equipped to make that all-important move from *me* to *we*.

This book will help couples navigate the new terrain of relationships in this era of entitlement and help put them back on track toward happily ever after, whether or not that makeup mirror on the wall is put away when Jake and Lydia say good night.

Part I

The Selfish Game

Chapter 1

Are You a Giver or a Taker?

THE FIRST TIME LYDIA AND JAKE WENT OUT TO DINNER, JAKE couldn't decide which flowers to choose, so he brought her three different bouquets. The first time they spent the night together at Lydia's apartment, she spent her entire afternoon making a trail of daisy petals—the flowers in her favorite of the three bouquets—leading from the doorway, down the long hall, and to the bedroom. A few weeks later, Jake asked if he could bring his laundry over—he didn't have his own machines—and she said yes, of course, they could make love while their clothes got clean. Standing in front of the washing machine, they slowly undressed each other. Giggling and acting like strippers, they tossed each item into the swirling water. Lydia tried to lead him toward her couch in the next room, but they made it only as far as the half-broken kitchen chair. They were so into each other that it didn't matter where they were.

Now, suddenly, three years later, they can't even make it happen in their beautiful bedroom with the teal silk sheets and the quilt they bought on their honeymoon. They can't seem to find each other, and they definitely can't find those people they were back in Lydia's old apartment. She is so tired from her long days at work. As a pharmaceutical sales rep she is constantly traveling and she is always on. Some days she has four or five meetings. It takes all her energy to try to talk those doctors into using her company's meds. When she gets home she simply can't keep her guard up anymore. She doesn't want to have to think about anything. She just wants to fall into bed and be left alone. Why is Jake so obsessed with that stupid mirror? Doesn't he understand that she has so much to worry about already? Lately, she finds herself wondering if she might have missed something in those early days. Did she marry the most selfish man on earth?

Jake is under a lot of pressure since he started taking classes at night in addition to his job. He needs some support at home. Why is Lydia thinking only of herself? How hard is it to keep his request in mind?

In my more than twenty years of relationship counseling, I've witnessed people asking these same questions again and again: "Do I live with the most selfish person alive?" "Am I being selfish when I do the things I want to do?" The line is muddled. People are plagued with guilt about asserting their own needs as well as balancing those needs with taking on and responding to those of their partners.

When is it okay to stand up for your needs? Is it possible to do so without feeling guilty? Should you sacrifice what you want and surrender your needs to meet those of your partner? Is it possible to do that without feeling resentful? Everyone is searching for the answers, but they don't know where to look.

To begin exploring the Selfish Game, and how it slowly creeps into relationships, chipping away at the notion of *we* and *us* and eventually pitting two once-loving partners against each other, let's first define selfishness. According to Webster's, *selfish* means "concerned excessively or exclusively with oneself: seeking or concentrating on one's own advantage, pleasure, or well-being without regard for others."

Oscar Wilde said, "Selfishness is not living as one wishes to live, it is asking others to live as one wishes to live." This is similar to a joke my mother would say when she wanted me to go along with her: "Be reasonable. Do it my way." This is exactly what most people think of when they think of selfishness. It's controlling and negative, and someone has to sacrifice and give up what he wants in order to please the person being selfish.

That is true in some circumstances, but in order to fully understand selfishness, you have to understand that, just like the heat in your Thai takeout, there are varying levels of selfishness, and they're not all bad. The first part of the word—*self*—denotes that one is thinking of one's self. As infants, we learn to cry out to get our basic needs met. It's the only way to let our parents know when we need to be fed and get changed. If you look at it from this perspective, selfishness is a necessary trait. But over time, we ideally learn to manage our needs without throwing a temper tantrum. We experience the disappointment and reality that we can't have everything we want all the time. We have to share. However, many variables and factors interfere with what should be a very simple, basic learning experience. Throughout the course of development that leads us to become caring, healthy, loving adults, there are a vast array of interferences (illness, death, abandonment, divorce, and alcohol issues, to name a few) that can lead to issues of mistrust and deprivation, which in turn result in adults with varying degrees of selfishness.

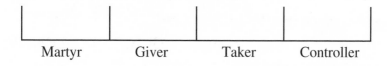

| Martyr | Giver | Taker | Controller |

If you want to rekindle the love you once had with your partner, or if you are looking to start fresh with a new partner and don't want to repeat past mistakes, it's imperative to discover where you and your partner fall on the selfishness scale to take your first step toward changing the Selfish Game.

There are four personality types that come into play. I'll define them below. You may see yourself or your partner in one type immediately or you may identify with a few different types. This is normal. Everyone has a dominant type, but that doesn't mean that you act out of that type 100 percent of the time. Take the short quiz that follows the definitions to help you determine where you fall on the continuum.

Over the years in my practice it has become clear to me that women are typically Martyrs and Givers (which is why I use women patients in those examples), but they can also be Takers and Controllers. Vice versa with men. Although men are typically Takers and Controllers, women can also play this role.

Martyr

Definition: Completely selfless. Martyrs will sacrifice their own needs in order to please their partner. Their sense of self is tied into the well-being of others, especially their significant other. Martyrs rarely express their own needs; it's easier for them to tend to others. They often feel powerless in relationships and tend to be stoic, suffering in silence.

Dominant emotion: Fear. The life of a Martyr is typically ruled by fear. They're afraid of upsetting their partner, making him angry, and losing his love. They don't verbalize what they want because they feel there is no point, that it won't make a difference anyway. They go along with what their partner wants, which creates a feeling of helplessness. Some find it to be a relief to go along with their partner's choices because they are clueless as to what they want, and they're afraid to make a decision for fear of making the wrong one. Martyrs tend to define themselves through their partner's world rather than acknowledge their own desires for fear of having to act on them, address them, or make room for them in the relationship. Martyrs are afraid of starting and doing things on their own, even if they're successful, accomplished people. The reality of their life is not in tandem with their fear of failure.

Catch phrase: "Of course. Whatever you want to do is fine with me."

When Monica first came into my office, she desperately wanted to get out of her marriage, but she was consumed with fear about it. She had a small child, was carrying the bulk of the household financial responsibility, and took care of the house. Her husband, Leonard, however, had all the power. He decided everything: what they ate for dinner, when and where they went out with friends, where they lived. Monica felt there was no room for her needs in the relationship.

This mentality worked fine in the beginning, because she told herself it didn't matter. As long as Leonard was happy, she was happy. But when she got pregnant, Leonard said to her, "You're the one who wants this baby. You can take care of it." It was a wake-up call: her relationship wasn't a partnership, and she was getting lost. She wanted out. But after years with Leonard, Monica felt emotionally insecure and unable to get on by herself, even though she was the breadwinner. She thought she couldn't do anything without him.

Monica began to realize other small behaviors that bothered her about Leonard. He would make statements like, "We really need to clean out the garage before this weekend." She understood that *we* really meant *you*. It was Leonard's way of telling her to do something and that he expected it to get done. She realized she nearly always went along with what Leonard wanted and expected, because making him happy and acquiescing was easier than not. But now she wanted to be able to voice her own opinion and make her own decisions, especially when it came to her children. She had had enough.

As I noted, like Monica, most Martyrs are women. However, that is not always the case. In chapter 7 you will meet Pete who, in an attempt to make his marriage to Julia work, sacrificed everything short of his right arm.

Giver

Definition: Somewhat selfless. Givers enjoy pleasing their partners. It makes them feel good, but it's not their only source of self-esteem. Oftentimes they are so generous that they overextend themselves. Because they give so much, that becomes the norm, and they often can feel taken advantage of and unappreciated.

Dominant emotion: Guilt. Unlike Martyrs, Givers understand that they do have choices in their relationship; they just typically make the choice to give more often than not. Because they want their partners to be happy, they feel guilty if they're pursuing their own needs. Givers can also be called people pleasers. They have a hard time saying no to others and yes to themselves.

Catch phrase: "What about me?"

When Laura and Jim came to see me, they were living together, and Laura was ready to get engaged, but Jim wasn't. She didn't understand why he was so hesitant to take their relationship to the next level, and she was very upset over it. She said she felt like she gave Jim everything, what more could she do to get him to commit? I instantly identified Laura as a Giver. In our first session, she said, "I love him and want to make him happy, but I feel like I'm doing everything he wants. I just wish he appreciated me."

If they were planning a vacation and were deciding whether to visit his family or hers, she would choose his, because she knew he expected that. One time she mentioned to Jim in the morning that she wanted him to go shopping with her that night to buy a wedding gift for their neighbors. But after dinner he decided to go out with friends. Other times they would agree early on that they would come home immediately following a movie, but as soon as they walked into the lobby, Jim would insist on getting a nightcap or dessert. She started to resent that he didn't hold true to the plans they had made. Jim would tell her that he was going to pay the bills, pick up the dry cleaning, or wash the dishes, and then he wouldn't. Laura would have to do her chores plus the ones he didn't do, because she wanted to make him happy and she wanted him to know she would be a great life partner. She planned their social calendar and always let him go out alone with his friends if he wanted to, but he wasn't coming around. Nothing was working.

They sought my help because Laura and Jim were trying to come to a sense of *we* as a couple—what would work for them in dealing with everybody else. They had gotten into a pattern. If Laura spoke up, Jim would say, "What's the big deal?" Laura would, in turn, feel as if she were blowing things out of proportion and being selfish by making a big to-do about it. But these little things added up and eventually began taking a toll on their relationship. Jim was unknowingly breaking up their sense of *we.*

Yet Jim had not realized Laura felt this way. He was shocked and offended when she called him selfish or said that they were anything less than very happy together. He didn't realize that

Laura gave in all the time, because she rarely said anything to him. He thought they were very happy together.

Givers, whether male or female, typically are the ones who keep the relationship on track—handling the responsibilities, the chores, the social calendar—but they often feel overburdened and can easily become distant or withdrawn from the relationship.

Laura had reached a point in the relationship where she still wanted Jim to be happy, but she was feeling walked all over more often than not and was becoming very resentful of Jim.

Taker

Definition: Takers expect to be given to and taken care of. They lead with being selfish. Takers focus on what they want as the norm. Occasionally they will factor in their partners, but usually only when their partner starts to make a fuss. Takers look to get their needs met in order to feel comfortable and secure in their world.

Dominant emotion: Disappointment. Takers are often disappointed when they don't get their own way, but they don't know how to tolerate that emotion. As a result, they are insistent on having their own way to avoid the disappointment of not getting what they want. They feel deserving, so they have no problem expecting the other person to go along with them. They, in fact, think that their partner should want to do things for them. They don't see themselves as selfish; they do feel that they're aware of their partner's needs and desires. They get their needs met by assuming and avoiding. They assume that their partner will want to do what they want to do. If not, they will work it out so that things go their way, whether it's directly by insisting or indirectly by manipulating through their behavior.

Catch phrase: "If you want to make me happy, then you will…"

Tina and Jerome had been married for only four months when they came to see me. Tina was ready to call it quits on her young marriage. She felt that everything in their life went by Jerome's clock: when to start a family, when to buy a new house, what to do on the weekends. Jerome was a Taker. He loved to go to hockey games and assumed that Tina would go with him, so he bought two season tickets. Tina tried to explain that there were so many other things she'd rather be doing, but Jerome got hurt and upset at that. He didn't understand why she didn't like going with him just to spend time with him. On the weekends, he liked to lie around and do nothing. Tina was a get-up-and-go kind of gal, but Jerome wouldn't budge. When she spoke up about what she wanted, Jerome responded with, "Don't you understand how hard I work? I need my downtime to relax. Don't you appreciate what I'm doing?"

She began to feel that his needs were taking up all the air in the relationship—even when it came to decorating their home. Jerome loved sports and had baseball memorabilia in every room. She didn't feel like he cared about her decorating style at all (which had nothing to do with balls). He was literally leaving no room for her self-expression on any level. As newlyweds, they were trying to establish a sense of *we,* but it was always all about Jerome.

Jerome wasn't dominating in personality, or even abrasive; he just walked around with an air of expectation and knew which buttons to push on Tina to get his way. He would easily get upset or offended if Tina had other ideas. Takers expect you to go along with them, and when you don't, they hit you with, "How could you be so selfish?"

Controller

Definition: Completely selfish. Controllers grab the spotlight in a relationship. The focus must always be on them, and if it's not, then they feel their partner doesn't love them. They're the important ones, their needs always come first, and nothing else matters. Controllers have the power and are thoughtless without realizing how it is affecting those around them. They're not even aware that their partner's needs exist. If they are aware, they view them as being selfish. Controllers always think that they're right and you're wrong. They want undivided attention and can get jealous if you're spending time with others. Anything that takes you away from them, whether it's resources or attention, is a problem for them.

Dominant emotion: Anger. When things don't go their way Controllers become very anxious and react in anger. Whereas Takers expect you to give to them, Controllers demand that you give to them. They are often insistent, overbearing, strong-willed, and relentless, wearing their partner down until they get their way. If their partner has needs that conflict with their own, they think their partner is the one being insensitive and selfish. They don't have any guilt about getting their needs met, because it's so vital, but they easily get hurt and upset and feel unloved if their partner doesn't meet their needs. Controllers also are quick to disconnect through anger if their partner doesn't listen to them, because the advice they offer is not meant as an option; it's a directive. Most Controllers have a way of doing things that makes them comfortable: how they put away the dishes, where they put their shoes, how low they will let their gas gauge get. If these things aren't done the way they want, Controllers will feel out of control and anxious, which is why what their partners do, eat, how often they call, etc., all become subject to their control. They often complain to their partner about what they don't like. Criticism and blame are their main tools of control. In a relationship with a Controller, any attempt to voice your opinion will turn into a power struggle, and you will get ignored or shut down.

Catch phrase: "It's all about me."

Gabe and Jenna had been married for three years, and she wanted a baby. Gabe told her that he wouldn't have one unless she guaranteed him that she would have sex with him a certain number of times each week. She thought Gabe was a total control freak.

Soon after they got married, he announced they were moving to Texas to be near his family. She countered with the point that they had never decided that together. She wouldn't budge, and he was infuriated. To this day, he has never let it go, and he continues to throw it in her face. He blames her for his unhappiness with living so far away from his family, and he holds it over her whenever he doesn't get what he wants in order to make her feel guilty and manipulate her into caving on other issues.

For two years Jenna was secretly coming to therapy. It was easier for her to avoid a confrontation with Gabe than to tell him the truth. When she finally decided to talk to Gabe about it, he was livid. "Why do you need to talk to anyone but me about your problems?" he asked.

When it comes to money, Gabe controls the purse strings. He chooses what they will and won't spend money on and pays the bills, and Jenna never makes any of the decisions, even though she contributes to the household income. Yet Gabe will still make comments that "they" need to watch their budget. "What am I supposed to watch?" Jenna asked me. "I don't spend any of the money."

Gabe is a classic Controller. He uses power, money, and anger to make Jenna feel insecure, frightened, and guilty so he can easily get his own way.

Take This Quiz
Are You a Martyr, Giver, Taker, or Controller?

With just eleven questions addressing the two primary areas of selfishness—sexual and emotional—you can determine where on the continuum you fall. If you're in a relationship, this will help you clarify your role in that relationship and how that plays into the way you interact with your partner.

1. After a long, lazy lovemaking session, you've just had a glorious orgasm. Unfortunately he's had a few glasses of wine and still hasn't climaxed. You're tired and sore, and Patrick Dempsey is on Letterman, and you want to watch. You:
    a. Continue for as long as it takes. If he doesn't have an orgasm, yours doesn't count for much.

b. Casually ask him, "Was it good for you?" as you reach for the remote control.

c. Continue for a while, and then suggest that he play with himself and you'll watch.

d. Continue until he climaxes, then mutter under your breath, "Geez, I've already missed half the interview. Thanks a lot."

2. The words that come to mind when you think about sex with your partner are:

a. "Oh, that feels great. Wait, let me do that to you."

b. "Yeah, just keep doing that, that's just what I like."

c. "My pleasure comes from giving you satisfaction."

d. "I just read about this great new move. Let's try doing it."

3. Despite repeated appeals, your husband continues to fall asleep promptly at ten o'clock each night and wakes up at six, eager to make love. Alas, you're not a morning person. In order to maintain your sex life, you:

a. Wake him up at eleven o'clock when you get in bed. If he wants to have sex, you've got to do it at a reasonable hour.

b. Set your alarm clock for six and have sex while you're still half asleep.

c. Ask him if he remembers that old tune from the seventies, "Afternoon Delight"? Maybe that's the best compromise...

     d. Take a stand and refuse to have sex with him. You know it won't be long until he gives in to your schedule.

4. When it comes to planning your annual vacation with your partner, you:

     a. Choose where you are going to go, buy the tickets, and tell your partner when he needs to take off work.

     b. Book another cruise. You're sick of them, but it's your partner's favorite way to travel.

     c. Ask your partner if he doesn't mind visiting your parents this year.

     d. Ask your partner where he wants to go. If he's happy, you're happy.

5. Your partner is a little bit of a clean freak and told you that he can't stand when you leave dirty dishes in the sink. You:

     a. Make an effort to put them in the dishwasher when you have the time.

     b. Leave them there. It's his problem that he's so OCD, not yours.

     c. Make sure you never leave dirty dishes in the sink again. You hate the idea of his being upset with you.

     d. Tell him you'll try, but leaving dishes in the sink is a lifelong habit, and you don't think it's really anything to get so upset about.

6. Your husband was late getting home from a weeklong business trip, and now the steak is cold and the wine is warm. You two had agreed to have a romantic dinner and discuss some important issues in your relationship, but when he walks through the door, he's horny and not in the mood to talk about anything. You:

   a. Are hurt that he doesn't acknowledge the dinner but go straight to bed with him. Maybe tomorrow he'll remember the talk you were supposed to have.

   b. Hop into bed and make love after making him promise you'll talk first thing in the morning. If he's hungry afterward, you might even heat up the steak.

   c. Relent but make it quite clear that you're going to talk after sex.

   d. Insist on talking or refuse to have sex.

7. You're waiting for an important call from your boss about a big deal at work. Your husband has planned a romantic dinner and asks you to leave your phone at home so you can concentrate on each other without any distractions. You:

   a. Send a quick email to your boss and let her know you'll be unavailable for the next two hours.

   b. Get really angry. How can your husband not understand how important this call is? Tell him you'll go to dinner, but you'll be taking your phone.

c. Tell him you love the gesture but sweetly ask if you can postpone your plans for another night. This call is really important.

d. Go to dinner with him but bring your phone and secretly check it in the bathroom throughout the night. You just can't miss this call.

8. Your husband buys you a new perfume that you don't especially like. You:

a. Wear it when he's around but put on your own favorite when he's not.

b. Tell him, "I really don't like this too much. Why don't you exchange it for that bottle of Obsession I love so much?"

c. Try it, hate it, wear it anyway. You don't want to seem ungrateful.

d. Tell him you appreciate the gesture. Then set it on your bathroom counter and let it collect dust.

9. You like to sleep with the fan on, but your husband gets cold easily and hates the noise that it makes. You:

a. Buy him earplugs and extra blankets for his side of the bed.

b. Leave it off. You'd rather he be comfortable.

c. Tell him to sleep in the guest room. You just can't get a good night's rest unless the fan is on.

d. You sleep in the guest room with the fan on. It really isn't fair to put him out.

10. What a shock! Your couch-potato spouse just bought himself a new suit, shaved his beard, and signed both of you up at a health club. What does it all mean?

    a. You don't know and you don't care. You can ill afford the suit, you liked his beard the way it was, and you're not about to start sweating. You have enough work to do already.

    b. Hmm, he looks good. Maybe you could give the StairMaster a try, just to see what happens. You might not go every day, but at least the two of you could go to the gym together a couple of days a week.

    c. Uh-oh. Obviously he's trying to tell you something. He's going for a total image overhaul, and you'd better learn to keep up with him. Or else.

    d. You feel a little put out. He should have conferred with you before making all these changes. You two need to have a serious conversation.

11. It's Tuesday night and you're geared up for *American Idol,* but there's a program about shark attacks on the Discovery Channel that your husband has been dying to see. You haven't seen your husband much this week and were really looking forward to snuggling with him on the couch and making fun of the bad singers. You:

    a. Turn to the Discovery Channel and TiVo *American Idol.* At least you'll get to snuggle with him, and you can watch your show later when you have time.

b. Tell him you've been looking forward to *Idol* all day. He can watch it with you or watch his show in your bedroom, but you're not budging.

c. Watch the Discovery Channel, but flip back to *Idol* during the commercials. You want to at least be able to join some of the watercooler gossip at work tomorrow.

d. Watch *Idol* and demand that he watch it with you. You've had this night planned in your mind all day, and he isn't going to ruin it for you.

SCORING

Give yourself the points as follows.

1.   a. 1 (M)   b. 4 (C)   c. 3 (T)   d. 2 (G)
2.   a. 2 (G)   b. 4 (C)   c. 1 (M)   d. 3 (T)
3.   a. 3 (T)   b. 1 (M)   c. 2 (G)   d. 4 (C)
4.   a. 4 (C)   b. 1 (M)   c. 3 (T)   d. 2 (G)
5.   a. 2 (G)   b. 4 (C)   c. 1 (M)   d. 3 (T)
6.   a. 1 (M)   b. 2 (G)   c. 3 (T)   d. 4 (C)
7.   a. 1 (M)   b. 4 (C)   c. 2 (G)   d. 3 (T)
8.   a. 2 (G)   b. 4 (C)   c. 1 (M)   d. 3 (T)
9.   a. 3 (T)   b. 1 (M)   c. 4 (C)   d. 2 (G)
10. a. 4 (C)   b. 2 (G)   c. 1 (M)   d. 3 (T)
11. a. 1 (M)   b. 3 (T)   c. 2 (G)   d. 4 (C)

Tally up your score and then refer to the chart below to determine your selfishness profile.

17 and below: Martyr

18–27: Giver
28–37: Taker
38–44: Controller

Now that you've pinpointed what the root of your personality type is, here's what you will learn in this book in order to create a healthier and happier relationship.

If you're a Martyr, then you will learn how to be true to yourself so you can stand up for your needs and have the courage to follow through on the things that are important to you on a day-to-day basis. You don't have to end a relationship in order to focus on your wants and desires. You will learn how to face the fear of your partner's being angry with you in a way that helps you become stronger rather than weaker. You will begin to appreciate that you do have a choice for yourself about your needs and that sometimes you will give, but that it's essential for you to take too. This is easier said than done, because a lot of Martyrs experience discomfort and difficulty accepting somebody doing things for them. You'll learn why it's so difficult, and more important, you'll learn how to do it.

If you're a Giver, then you will learn how to manage your guilt more constructively so you're not giving in to your partner at the expense of yourself. You will learn when it's important to say yes to yourself and when it's more important to do things for your partner out of love and caring. When you choose to give to yourself, you will learn how to do it without guilt interfering. You'll also learn how to identify your needs and distinguish which are vital, so you can pick and choose the issues you stand up for.

If you're a Taker, you will learn that the other person also has a right to expect certain things and have their needs met. The first step is learning how to tolerate being disappointed and not have things always work out your way. You will balance that with a more realistic understanding that relationships are about give and take. You will learn to accept that there will be times when you're not going to get what you want, but it will be balanced by the times that you will. You will learn to experience the pleasure of sharing and making the other person happy as a way to also feel good for yourself. And you'll learn how to consider your partner's feelings and needs so you can include them when it comes to making decisions for yourself and the way that you behave. For Takers, it's all about consideration—and the fact that they rarely have any.

If you're a Controller, you will learn how to manage your anxiety by developing boundaries around your behaviors and that of your significant other so you can learn to pull back and step out of your partner's business. Even though you like things a certain way, you'll start to learn how to make room and give respect to the differences in your and your partner's needs. You'll learn how to tolerate those differences without personalizing everything and turning it into proof that the person doesn't love you.

So how do these types play out in your relationship? There are basically three combinations that you can have. Typically and hopefully, there is a complementarity of roles. For instance, if you are naturally a Giver, you will probably seek out a Taker or a Controller. But there are instances when Takers/Controllers pair with other Takers/Controllers and Givers/Martyrs pair with other

Givers/Martyrs. The different pairings determine how much active conflict, battle, and rage are present in a relationship, as well as how much avoidance, distance, and disconnect are present. Ideally, both people in the relationship will be a little bit giving and a little bit taking at alternate times. With that healthy balance comes trust that when you give, you will receive. When you meet needs, your needs will be met.

With an imbalance, your relationship will fall into one of these categories:

1. Martyr/Giver and Taker/Controller

   In this pairing, the Taker/Controller is typically running the show while the Martyr/Giver goes along for the ride. This pairing can work for a short period of time, until the Martyr/Giver comes to the realization that none of their needs are getting met. That's when conflict can begin, power struggles take shape, and the Martyr/Giver will either withdraw and seek ways to end the relationship or start to learn (most likely through therapy) how to stand up for themselves.

2. Martyr/Giver and Martyr/Giver

   The struggle with this partnership is that in each person's effort to always please the other person, it's hard for them to be true to themselves and voice their own needs. Misunderstanding and miscommunication abound, creating resentment and anger that never gets expressed. Each partner likely feels guilt, and the relationship winds up feeling empty and void of real happiness because neither person is sure about what is going to make them happy. Each partner is attempting to make the other person happy without consideration of their own happiness. In this matchup, there is little to no conflict, but both partners are likely not getting their needs met. When it comes time to choose what to do on a Saturday night, they both look at each other and say, "What do you want to do?" Neither partner wants to assert their wishes in fear of it not being what their partner wants to do. This can be a very empty relationship that lacks communication and true happiness for either partner.

3. Taker/Controller and Taker/Controller

    In this pairing, one person might be voicing criticism and demands deliberately, and the other person might be extremely manipulative or unresponsive. There's a back-and-forth of being upset with each other's behaviors. They're always complaining and arguing about the other person's behaviors, either what they did or didn't do. This is an explosive matchup that is a constant power struggle, where both partners are jockeying to get their needs met. Little consideration is taken for the other, and both people are out for themselves, whether it's what temperature to set the thermostat at or where to go on vacation. Battles will rage on in this relationship until they become tired of the constant conflict and seek resolution.

Your personality type and how it plays out in your relationship dictates the expectations you have of yourself and your partner and what it means to be a part of your couplehood. The roots of many of these expectations can be traced back to long before you knew your partner, and your partner's to long before they knew you. All of this determines the way you communicate your needs to your partner—or don't communicate them, as the case may be. Your communication styles predict whether you're engaging in all-out angry battle or silent cold wars. You can see, there is a lot going on here. In chapter 2, you'll discover what your expectations are, where they come from, and how your communication styles may be traced back to your family. All of this will help you on your journey from becoming a *me* to a *we* with your partner.

Chapter 2

If You Loved Me, You Would...

The Great Expectation

As I said, nobody gets a pass on doing the work. Not even me!

When my husband Marc and I were on our honeymoon in Greece, we had one of the best margherita pizzas I have ever had. It had a thin luscious crust, wonderful tomato sauce that tasted like the Greek sun, and creamy mozzarella. We savored it.

I was about to take my last bite. It was a little bit of everything toward the back of the slice so it would include a salty bubble of crust.

"Can I have that?" my new husband said from across the table.

"What, my last bite?" I asked incredulously. "No way."

Not only was I surprised by his question, but I was even more surprised by his reaction. He got angry. He could not believe that I wouldn't give him my last bite. What was going on here? In my family, we shared food all the time, but we each relished our last bites. That last bite was off-limits. Nobody in my family would ever ask for it. What could it mean that my new spouse was asking me for it now and that he was so angry that I didn't give it to him? Hadn't he already had his own final bite? Why did he want mine; why did he need more?

There it was: the judgment mirror. Marc's mirror told me I was being stingy. And what Marc was seeing in my judgment mirror was that I thought he was being greedy. At that moment, we were no longer being seen through the other's eyes of love and neither of us liked what we saw. Naturally, we survived the argument, and dealt with it largely by using humor—joking regularly about his last bite or my last bite. But for a long time, neither of us understood the other's feelings.

A few years later we were at the shore with Marc's sister Carol and his brother Jack. We were out on the deck, eating scrumptious tuna fish sandwiches with red onion and dill, when Jack gave Carol a look. Without a word, she leaned over and handed him her last bite. My mouth dropped.

"Carol, he just took your last bite!" I said.

"Well," she said, clearly not bothered. "That's how we say 'I love you.'"

"What do you mean by that?" I replied.

"I know how much it means to him to eat my last bite, so that makes me happy to give it to him," she explained.

A light bulb went on for me. In Marc's family, sharing your last bite was an expression of love. In the same way that people show love by being affectionate with a hug or a tickle or buying presents, being willing to give away a last bite was their way of doing just that. And suddenly I was back in Greece, sitting at the table across from Marc with the last bite of pizza in my hand. My unwillingness to give it to him meant, as far as he was concerned, that I didn't love him enough. In that moment on our honeymoon, a lot transpired. Based on how we experienced love as children, we were judging each other's actions and interpreting them to mean that each of us was being selfish because we weren't being given love the way we were used to getting it. I couldn't understand how he could ask me to give up something that was so important to me. Marc couldn't understand why I wasn't willing to do something that meant a lot and felt so natural to him.

Recently I watched the movie *Julie and Julia* and had to laugh when Julia Child and her husband Paul were enjoying a meal at a French restaurant and she cooed to him something like, "I love you so much you can have my first bite." Funny, those bites— whether they're the last ones or the first ones—are crucial. It doesn't matter if they come at the beginning or the end of the meal; what matters is what it means to you.

It boils down to this: If you loved me, you would... If you loved me, you would give me your last bite. If you loved me, you would respect and understand the way I handle my anger. If you loved me, you would visit my parents. If you loved me, you would agree to have three children. If you loved me, you would give my sister a break. The list goes on and on. What you will come to see with the tools you gain in this book is that many of your partner's seemingly selfish actions have nothing to do with how much he loves you, and the fact that you are judging his behavior in this way is putting enough pressure on your relationship to cook a duck.

The needs we all have, these things that we grow to expect, come directly out of the way we grew up and the families we grew up with. And, of course, the likelihood that your partner grew up in a family just like yours is minimal. Maybe you grew up in a big family with four brothers, but your husband was an only child. So often we look to replicate our families. You want a big family with five children. He loved his cozy, calm house of three and thinks having an only child is a good idea. How do you reconcile this? Or maybe you and your partner talked about having a family before you were married. In your mind, that obviously meant three kids, but in his mind that clearly meant two. After your second child is born, your husband thinks your family is complete. Didn't you agree to that when you talked about having a family together so long ago? Uh-oh. No, you didn't. Didn't he agree to three?

Or his family members curse like drunken sailors—all the time—and it doesn't mean a thing to him. But in your house, your mother slapped you on the thigh any time you uttered a word that she didn't like, and that included the word *crap*. So you associate any curse word with a stinging feeling, and it makes you wince. Every time your husband says one of those words—when he drops his napkin in the floor, when his football team doesn't score, when he misses a parking spot—you cringe. You ask him to watch his language, but this is how he has been talking his entire life. He tells you to lighten up, but you can barely stand it.

This was the case with Lacey and Chase when they came to see me. Lacey grew up in a family where cursing and name-calling was the norm. Chase, on the other hand, came from a family that completely shut down emotionally when someone's feelings were hurt. So they got into a bad cycle: Lacey called Chase names—asshole, jerk—without even thinking. She did this when he didn't make the bed or left the milk out on the counter all day. She did this when she was angry, if she thought he looked a little too long at the pretty waitress at their favorite Japanese restaurant. And Chase would have no reaction; he would immediately withdraw into himself and avoid all conversation.

By the time they sought my help, Lacey wanted to end the marriage. She couldn't stand the way he gave her the silent treatment, sometimes for days, for no real reason. It was so strange. Was there something wrong with him? He was always sulking, acting like his feelings were hurt. She couldn't figure out why.

But Chase disagreed. He told her many times that her name-calling bothered him, but it just didn't seem to sink in. On many occasions he asked her to clean up her mouth, to think before she said something mean. There were times, he admitted, when she said she was sorry, but within an hour she would be doing it again. He couldn't stand it anymore and stopped even trying to explain what he was upset about.

The judgment mirror that Lacey held up to Chase showed clearly that she felt he was acting like a baby. Couldn't he take it and get over it? And the judgment mirror that he held up to her reflected his judgment that she was vulgar.

In Lacey's family, they all spoke to each other this way—calling each other idiot and moron and saying shut up and piss off. Once it was said, that was it. It was done. No hard feelings. In Chase's family, however, there had been none of that. His mother was controlling but rarely raised her voice. If she was disappointed or wanted to punish Chase, she simply withdrew. That was the way they coped, and so that is the way he learned to communicate his disapproval.

One afternoon, Lacey fell down the stairs and knew she had to go to the emergency room—her shoulder was on fire. This happened two days into a stretch of Chase's not speaking to her. When she called his cell phone, he didn't answer. She tried again. Still nothing. She texted him, "911," and waited. No response. She finally dragged herself to a neighbor's house, and the neighbor called an ambulance because she was too freaked out to drive Lacey to the hospital herself. Lacey's arm was practically dangling. That was the last straw. How could Lacey depend on Chase? She couldn't. She had had it.

The power of our family and how we grew up have a huge impact on how we think things should be. Our sense of normal comes directly from that place. It undercuts everything we want, believe, and do and leads directly to the belief: If you loved me, you would..., because my family did.

This is at the core of all Selfish Hot Spots—those insidious disagreements that come up over and over again in a relationship. You pay more attention to your iPhone than you do to me. You never call when you say you will. You never say you love me. You are pushing me so hard about starting a family. You never buy me a birthday present. You always want to spend our precious vacation time with your family. Whatever it is in your relationship that comes up repeatedly with no resolution, causing anger and sadness every time it rears its ugly head, is a Selfish Hot Spot. We will explore Selfish Hot Spots fully in the next chapter, but as you read this chapter and maybe even recognize yourself in some of these examples, keep the idea of the Selfish Hot Spot in mind. It is at the core of the Selfish Game.

Consider Rose and Augustine. He cannot control his anger. His temper flares at the seemingly smallest things. The minute he isn't happy, his voice gets louder and louder, and he lashes out in anger and blames Rose. It's how he communicates. Rose had an idea about this before they got married. She had seen him with his brothers, and they could get into heated fights with all three of them screaming at each other, but she figured that was just the way the brothers interacted.

She and Augustine met, fell in love, and got married in less than six months. Those were blissful months. Looking back, she can't think of a single disagreement they had. It was so easy to get along. What was there to work out, anyway? Where to have dinner? Which park to ride their bikes in on a beautiful Saturday? How many times to make love in one day? At just the moment he was thinking how nice it would be to have sex, she would reach over and brush her hand along his crotch. A few hours later she would be surprised to find herself horny again, and there he would be, kissing her behind her ears, massaging her butt. They seemed to want exactly the same things at exactly the same times.

The first time Rose heard Augustine's voice sound the way it does when he fights with his brothers, although they were nowhere in sight, was on the way back from their honeymoon in St. Croix. The journey there had been easy, the flight empty and smooth. But there was a storm brewing when they left the island a week later. The skies were dark, and the palm trees were blowing in the strong wind. The line at the gate was getting longer and longer. Everyone was trying to get out immediately, before the storm truly hit, so the plane looked like it was going to be packed. Rose didn't mind, she trusted the airline would make the right decision about whether to fly or not, and she knew they had assigned seats. But Augustine was panicked—he hated flying to begin with. Throw in a storm and a crowd, and his nerve level rose to the moon. As they finally boarded and found their seats, Augustine pushed past Rose and took the window seat.

"I want to sit there," she said, smiling, holding up her camera. "I want to see all the places we were on St. Croix as we take off, if I can find them."

"What, are you kidding?" he barked in a voice she didn't recognize. "I'm sitting here."

"Come on, honey, let me," she tried again.

"I told you we never should have come to this island," Augustine said nastily. "Now shut up, sit down, and don't talk to me until we land."

Oh, she recognized *that* voice. It was the one he used with his brothers. After that, gradually, the anger crept into their day-to-day lives. For a long time, Rose was surprised by it each time it showed up, then she came to expect it and reacted before she even heard it. What was wrong with him? Who yells so much and blames everyone for everything? Her family never spoke to each other that way. Never! In her family, if you were mad or you didn't get what you wanted, you excused yourself from the situation. Later, maybe, you would mention it casually so you could better understand what had happened. And by then the other person had a chance to think about it too, and a restorative conversation almost always followed. But Augustine's family seemed to be angry all the time. The first time they were in the car with his parents and his father was driving, Augustine's mother screamed the whole time. "No! Turn left!" "Slow down! What is wrong with you?" "That's a stop sign. How could you not have seen that?"

So Rose started to get scared. She had no idea Augustine was this way. She should have taken more time to get to know him before they got married. What had she been thinking? Slowly, she withdrew. It was the only way she knew of to deal with her feelings and the conflict with her husband. She retreated, the way she always did growing up, but the calm support she found with her parents and siblings just wasn't there with Augustine. There was no way to get out of the hole.

Augustine, on the other hand, could not understand what Rose's problem was. He was acting the way he always did. It seemed completely normal to him. He didn't yell more than most people. He wasn't blaming her for anything. What was she talking about? Everyone yelled like this. You had to act that way to get what you wanted. It didn't mean he didn't love her. Of course not! Hell, she should hear his father yell. She was being ridiculous. He just couldn't figure it out.

Again, the judgment mirrors. Hers reflected that he was acting inappropriately and appeared crazy. His showed that she was being way too sensitive. When people come into my office, at some point or another, they are going to hurl these accusations at each other.

Another way these expectations manifest themselves in Selfish Hot Spots is the way one partner's family deals with taking care of other family members versus the way the other one does. Take Chloe and Abe, for example. Chloe grew up in a house where family came above all else. When someone was sick, you would drop everything to spend long hours in the hospital or at home to care for them.

She spent much of her life with one uncle or aunt living with them at different times. Her mom's sister lived with them after she got divorced, bringing her young son along. She was there for more than a year, staying in the guest room and chipping in with the cooking and the errands. She was absorbed into the family until she could get on her feet. One time, her father's brother spent six months with them after leaving a rehab center, which followed a hospital stay to recover from alcohol poisoning. His parents lived too far from his therapist, so Chloe's parents invited him in. She remembers sitting with her uncle, reading *The Secret*

Garden, and how he would sneak her Swedish Fish whenever he got a chance. She loved having her aunt and uncle live with them when she was little. It made her family richer.

Abe's family, on the other hand, kept to itself. If someone was sick, you would make a token visit and then you could get on with your day. They rarely had houseguests, even for a night or two. His mother intentionally did not set up the extra room as a guest room so it would not be easy for people to come stay. "If people want to visit, they can pay for a hotel," she often said. When Abe's grandmother got sick and couldn't live alone anymore, there was no discussion about having her live with them, even though they had the room. They found a well-run nursing home, arranged her admittance, and helped her move in. They visited her once a week, for one hour on Sunday afternoons. Abe's father made it clear that their house was their house and nobody else's.

When Chloe's mother got thyroid cancer, Chloe wanted her to live with them while she recovered from surgery. Her father had died, and her mother was alone. But Abe said no, everyone should live in their own house. He pointed out that she had friends and a support network that they would never be able to duplicate. When they found out that one of the great hospitals with everything she needed for her follow-up treatment was just twenty miles away from their house—not to mention they had a big empty room with its own bathroom on a separate floor from their own room—Abe still said no. He pointed out that he had just spent days in the hospital visiting her mother. Wasn't that enough? He needed his own space. Chloe was heartbroken.

The way they each grew up was what they each thought was normal. How would they get beyond this and come to some agreement? If Abe refuses, Chloe will never forgive him if something worse happens to her mother, for example, if she's lonely or if the doctors near her house can't help. She will always wonder if things might have been different. Abe, on the other hand, doesn't think it's right to invite anyone beyond your immediate family to live with you. It is just not done that way. Chloe thinks, if you loved me, you would let my mother come live with us. Abe thinks, if you loved me, you would never ask such a thing.

For Sofia and Scott, everything seems to revolve around Scott's younger sister Hazel, and Sofia isn't sure how much longer she'll be able to stand it. When Scott and she first started dating, she was well aware of the concessions everyone made for Hazel. On more than one occasion, they drove all the way to Westchester to pick her up and bring her back into the city, even though it would have been seemingly easy for her to take the train. There was a strange sense of responsibility that Scott felt toward Hazel, and Sofia simply didn't understand it. She knew he did much of it to please and help his parents, who worried excessively about Hazel. But still!

It soon became clear that it was much worse than she realized. Everyone tiptoed around Hazel. Her preferences always ruled. If things didn't go her way, she became immediately angry. But it was more than that. They all seemed terrified that one false move would drive her away. There were times recently when Sofia thought to herself, *Would that really be so bad?* But for Scott and

38

his parents the answer was apparently a resounding yes. As far as Scott and his family were concerned, whatever Hazel wanted, Hazel should have. Even when it came to Sofia and Scott's wedding! Hazel didn't like outdoor parties because she has bad allergies, so Sofia's dream of getting married on the banks of the Hudson River was not even an option.

Now, it seemed, Hazel was seeping into every corner of their lives. His parents liked to gather the family together almost every weekend for a big brunch, but Hazel would wait until the last minute to commit to which day. She had just gotten out of a bad relationship, and she said that she had to remain open in case one of her dating prospects came through. So every Saturday and Sunday they were on call for brunch and could never make any other plans. And when they did get together for brunch, Hazel expected to be catered to. She never helped bring things to the table or clean up, and nobody ever said a word about it.

To make things worse, Hazel started to call on whatever day they weren't having brunch to ask Scott to come to her apartment to install bookshelves or help her put down mouse traps. Sometimes, Hazel would call while they were relaxing in bed on a weekend morning, about to make love, and Scott would jump up and drive up to her place. Their leisurely romps were cut short or cut out completely, and once again Sofia felt like she was being completely pushed to the side.

Scott is what I call a Super Sibling. He does everything in his power to help his sister, and, as is often the case, he is largely motivated by his parents. For whatever reason, the Super Sibling and his parents are afraid the other sibling will remove himself or herself in anger from the family. They're afraid the other sibling won't be able to function without their help. Everyone goes along with their constant demands. This can cause tremendous resentment in a marriage when the Super Sibling's spouse feels that the other sibling is interfering with their lives.

Scott can't understand why Sofia is so angry about this. Hazel is his sister, for heaven's sake! When he married Sofia, he certainly thought that she held family to the same level of importance that he did. Why would she ask him to ignore Hazel's requests? She was still getting over her bad breakup; she doesn't have a spouse to rely on. Besides, he doesn't want his parents to worry so much. When Hazel gets into a snit and refuses to come to a brunch, or stops answering the phone, his parents become overly upset. Sometimes his father stops eating and sleeping, and once he drove through the night to get to Hazel's apartment even though his eyes aren't so great in the dark. Scott can't have that hanging over his head.

Roles become so clear and yet so convoluted. Scott is a Giver to his parents and his sister. Maybe, sometimes, like in situations when he and Sofia are about to make love, and he stops without a word if Hazel needs him, he might be considered a Martyr. But what about his role in his marriage? Clearly he is then a Taker when it comes to Sofia, at least when Hazel is involved. He does what he has to do, and he expects Sofia to understand and go along. In so many ways he is leveling the playing field of his life. This is what is expected of him, so, consequently, this is what is now expected of her. It can happen for so many reasons. With Scott and Hazel and their parents, it is a common conflict of needs. Throw in any additional problems a sibling might have—drug or alcohol abuse, a gambling problem, not being able to hold a job—and the toll on the others can be even greater. This behavior can develop out of a cultural expectation as well. (If you want to learn more about this relatively common phenomenon, I cover the topic completely in my book *Adult Sibling Rivalry*.)

Over and over I see people asking the questions that Sofia and Scott are asking about each other. Is her request more important than mine? How could I have missed this about my partner? Why doesn't he understand how important this is to me?

Sharon and Victor have also been asking these questions lately. They were living together, but Victor's entire way of conducting his time and activities conflicted with hers. She was very structured and liked to make plans, sometimes even knowing what she would be doing from hour to hour on a weekend day. He was the opposite, as loosey-goosey as you could get. He never wanted to make plans. He wanted to see where the day took him.

When they first started dating, Sharon thought this was romantic. She liked being pulled out of her everyday rigidity. But as soon as they moved in together, she started to think she had made a mistake. She and Victor would have plans to go to dinner, but five minutes before they were out the door, one of his buddies would stop by and thwart the whole plan. He would invite his buddy in, start a game of cards, offer him a beer, all the while Sharon would be ready and waiting near the door. When she complained, Victor kept telling her to lighten up.

Once, after they had gone to bed for the night, the phone rang. It was Victor's sister. She was driving through New York and needed a place to stay. She would be there in twenty minutes. Sharon was horrified. They were asleep! The house was not ready for a guest. She had to be up for a meeting in the morning. But Victor shook off all of her complaints and welcomed his sister who, it turned out, ended up staying for an entire week.

Sharon and Victor had constant battles over this. He would go out for a drink, promising to be home in an hour, and then he would show up four hours later. They would have plans to go to a movie, and at the last minute he would decide he would rather watch the football game that he just discovered was on TV.

Finally, a few days before her birthday weekend, Victor's family planned an impromptu birthday celebration for his father. Even though Sharon had been looking forward to the dinner they had planned at the hottest Italian bistro in town (she had to call two months in advance to get the reservation!), Victor wanted to change their plans so they could be with his family. Needless to say, Sharon and Victor grew up in very different households. His depended on spur of the moment decisions and loose plans and the idea that family comes first, no matter what. Hers was built on structure and dependability and the idea that sometimes other things are as important as family gatherings. His family expected him to be present at all functions, no matter how little warning anyone had, and they expected him to welcome a family member into his home with little or no notice. Sharon's family planned ahead. She always knew if someone was going to visit and exactly how long that person was going to stay. Birthday parties were decided on far in advance and neatly written on everyone's calendars. How can two such different people with such varying upbringings come together successfully and make their couple-hood work?

We'll get into the tools you'll need to do just that as we get deeper into the book. But before we move on to the next chapter—Selfish Hot Spots—there are a few items that fall under the expectation umbrella that I think are important to mention.

One is the idea of Why Do I Have to Ask? In other words, tell me if you have a problem or if you want me to do it a different way. Don't make me guess. Women often ask their husbands, Why do I always have to ask you to do something? Why can't you just do it? And men often counter this question with (1) you looked like you had it under control, how was I supposed to know you needed my help? Or (2) you like it done your way. The last time I loaded the dishwasher, you told me I put the mugs in the wrong place. A selfish scenario ensues, and so much of it goes back to what your own family did while you were growing up. Your mother always handled the kitchen after dinner—she wanted it that way—so it makes sense to you that your wife would want to do it too. Or your father was 100 percent responsible for making sure all batteries in all household gadgets were in working order. It isn't even something you think about.

Similarly, and for some of the same reasons, cars and maps are often at the center of heated disagreements. You don't want to drive—your mother rarely did—so your husband always does.

43

But he sometimes wonders, Why does this always fall to me? Or, in his childhood car, his mother was the navigator. She had a map at the ready all the time. But you have never been good with maps, plus you feel carsick when you look down while the car is moving. Your husband finds this very annoying. He will constantly ask you to look at the map. You don't even try. He ends up getting lost and sulking. You get mad because you never promised to be a good map reader! Why would he ever have thought that, and why would he think you might react differently from the way you did last week? This happens every time you drive someplace new, as though it is happening for the first time, or your partner thinks you are going to reset and suddenly want to drive or suddenly become good at reading a map. Every time, you and your partner end up thinking, "If you loved me, you would…" And it isn't only cars and maps. This is a common problem. One of the many things you will learn from this book is how to handle this situation in a different way, thereby stopping the repetitive negative behavior.

Now let's talk about expectations with a capital *E*. The ones we pretty much count on when we say, "For better or worse, in sickness and in health." Most people who are married said those words or similar words when they made the marriage official, but you would be hard pressed to find someone who didn't expect that "for better" and "in health" would win out. So what happens when things don't turn out the way you hoped they would? When things aren't as good as they once were because your spouse loses his job. Or what if someone gets sick? Well, that would be hard enough to deal with. But if the couple is already dealing with Selfish Hot Spots of any sort, and they don't have the proper tools to sort those out, it will be that much harder to deal with the unexpected.

When Emily and Ned decided to get married, their lives seemed perfect. They were tall, handsome people. He was a successful lawyer on the road to being a partner in a well-known firm. She had just opened her own corner bakery with the help of her parents. Her pumpkin cupcakes with toffee icing had just been written up in the newspaper as the best in the city. They had a nice car and a great apartment on the seventeenth floor of an elegant building. Three years later, when they decided to try to get pregnant, they did. Right away. And nine months after that they had their first daughter. Then they moved into a house on a block they always dreamed about living on. They redid their kitchen to make it perfect—all yellow and blue. Two years later they got pregnant again. And two months after that Ned's law firm closed.

Now they had two kids, a mortgage that was just slightly above what they should really be paying each month, and Emily had just signed a lease to open a second bakery across town. At first it seemed like it might be okay. Ned is a great lawyer; he should be able to find a job quickly. But it turned out that he didn't really try so hard. He kept saying he would, but time and time again, Emily would find him starting a new project on the house or sitting in bed and listening to his iPod. Suddenly all the things that didn't seem so bad before—the way he always wanted to talk when she was busy planning next week's recipes, or the way he never really took charge of anything, not their vacations or their meals or, now, their future—started to get under her skin. After three months of his being out of work, she could barely stand to be in the house with him at the same time. She started making excuses, leaving him with the kids more and more.

Ned couldn't understand it. Sure, things weren't as great as they had once been, but wasn't your wife supposed to stand by you when you're down? So, what if he needed a little time to get over the shock of losing his job? He thought that was going to be the job of a lifetime. He needed a little perspective, a few months to change gears. He was so happy when she was home. He would follow her from room to room, ask about the bakery, hope she might offer some help with his résumé or job search. It took him a while before he realized she was there less and less. She rarely smiled when he came into the room anymore. When was the last time she kissed him hello or good-bye? When was the last time they had sex?

Ned still hoped to see the admiration, respect, and love that was so present at the beginning of their relationship reflected back at him, but all he saw was the opposite. In the same way that their wedding vows were so hopeful and uplifting, so was that initial reflection from her mirror of romance. It always starts out that way.

Losing a job happens. If you're lucky, and your marriage is long, you're going to encounter some unexpected obstacles along the way. The stronger you are, regardless of how many Selfish Hot Spots you have, the better you'll be able to deal with them.

Much of what I'm talking about here operates under the surface. You aren't always thinking, *He had three brothers, so what does that mean?* Or, *My mother likes to plan birthday parties six months in advance; how is that going to affect my marriage?* But it is always there, and when a problem does surface, people don't know how to handle it. Most people don't have the talking tools to get to a resolution. As we move through this book, we are going to find them together. But first, let's talk about those nasty Selfish Hot Spots. Get comfortable on the couch. I'm sure you'll recognize a few.

Chapter 3

Selfish Hot Spots

WHEN JAKE'S FRIEND TIM CALLS LATE ONE AFTERNOON TO invite him to a hockey game that night, Jake's first thought is no, he shouldn't. He was out the night before at class, and Lydia told him that morning that she planned to cook a nice dinner tonight. She even came over to him and kissed him after she said it. He thinks it is going to be some sort of Chinese pork roast, or maybe it's linguine with white clams—he wasn't really listening.

"Come on, man," Tim urges. "It'll be fun. I'm buying the beers."

Why shouldn't he? Jake thinks to himself. He didn't ask Lydia to make dinner, and to be perfectly honest, he doesn't feel like going home right after work. Class was stressful last night. He could use a break.

"Sure, thanks," he hears himself say, already thinking ahead to how he's going to deal with Lydia's undoubtedly angry response. She's probably already at home beginning project romantic dinner, as she said with a wink this morning. How stupid.

"Great, I'll pick you up around six," Tim says. Jake murmurs in agreement and then hangs up the phone. He thinks about calling Lydia right away but decides he'll wait until later. She's at home cooking, doing exactly what she wants to do, and she didn't even ask if he wanted her to. Maybe he would have preferred to go out to dinner. Why shouldn't he get to do what he wants? Besides, the last three times he wanted to have sex with her, she didn't want to. He didn't feel so bad about this, after all.

It is hard to imagine, impossible even, that habits your partner has or choices she makes will affect you in this way when you first begin your relationship together. Along the same lines, you would never have believed that some of the things you do, which seem so unimportant to you, might bother her so much. You begin a relationship thinking you'll be immune to any of those problems. You will never let anything come between you and your partner. And then…

Of course, most people don't enter a relationship with the intention of making their partner miserable. I say that first and foremost because it's important to dismantle the belief that all selfish behavior is deliberate and intentionally hurtful. Let's say that you get upset and angry that your husband habitually runs late or won't visit your parents or spends more time on his iPhone than he spends talking to you. Yes, these are selfish, infuriating behaviors, but they're not necessarily aimed at you. In other words, your partner doesn't decide to be late in order to intentionally hurt you. You see his behavior as being rude, thoughtless, and inconsiderate, but he probably doesn't share that belief. Most likely, he's clueless as to why you're so upset with him and why you would take these actions so personally. If it doesn't bother him, why does it bother you? More often than not, he has no understanding of the impact his behavior has on you and why you can't just accept it and adjust to it. Does that sound familiar? This isn't to excuse or dismiss selfish behavior; this is to help you gain insight into what drives your partner so you can derive more realistic expectations when it comes to your relationship.

That said, although selfish behavior isn't always personal, it's still hurtful, which is why it plays a big role in the demise of relationships. It can be hard to understand that your partner isn't behaving deliberately. If he knows something bothers you, why does he still do it? It feels like a personal attack. The reason you oftentimes get so upset is that you're working under the assumption that if you tell your partner that something bothers you, he will stop it. However, there are certain behaviors your partner may feel are out of his control—whether it's messiness, lateness, forgetfulness—and he's accepted those behaviors as part of his personality. He probably expects you to do the same, which is where the conflict comes in. He may even have great intentions to change, but in spite of himself, he can't seem to get past it. In that instance, you may feel maligned by his selfish behavior, and he may in turn feel unsupported by your inability to understand his behavior. It's a vicious cycle where both people feel hurt, and instead of being equipped to effectively communicate about the problem, nine out of ten times they will simply retaliate or attack each other with criticism.

These sticking points, the ones that seem to get in your way over and over again and stop you from moving forward with your partner, are Selfish Hot Spots—and you never know before you hit one that it is going to make such a mess. It could be anything from not cleaning up your shoes to not putting the orange juice where your wife thinks it should go in the refrigerator. It could also involve something much bigger: where to live in the world, what religion to raise your children, when to get married or move in together, and if and when to have a baby. Whatever it is, if it keeps trapping you in the quicksand, then it is a Selfish Hot Spot. It can consume you mentally and emotionally. It can fill you with rage, contempt, and disgust and leave you feeling continually disappointed.

Selfish Hot Spots fall into two categories: Big-Ticket Items and Paper Cuts. The Paper Cuts are the ones that really sneak up on you. Ouch! I can't believe that hurt so much, and it was just a piece of paper. We'll talk about many of these, but the truth is, they can be anything at all from that makeup mirror you keep hitting to how one partner handles the mail. The Big-Ticket Items, on the other hand, are just that: large life decisions that, when two people agree, can be quite smooth in the making. But when each member of the couple wants it a different way, these obstacles can make it almost impossible to move ahead. I want to look at a few of these major life decisions that are causing couples so much stress and lead to Selfish Standoffs in which both people dig their heels in, hold on to the belief that they are right, and refuse to back down.

Big-Ticket Items
Ready or Not?

Let's consider Alyssa and Kevin. They've been dating for almost two years, and Alyssa is starting to develop questions and doubts. To begin with, Kevin would not say he loved her for the longest time. She longed to hear it, was very open with her feelings toward him, and couldn't figure out what held him back. That far into a relationship, she was sure, he must have known if he loved her or not. They had already shared many of the things couples share as they become serious. They'd met each other's family. They spent a ton of time together at one or the other's apartment. But he would not say he loved her. After a year, he finally told her. But by then it was a festering wound, a "thing" between them. So, a few months later, when he started resisting the next step—to move in together and start thinking about getting married—it was already loaded. There he was again, dragging his feet.

All along Alyssa has tried to be supportive. She knows she loves him. She figures if she gives him time, he'll come around. But suddenly she isn't so sure, and she's spent months focused on him and worries that if he isn't the one, she's wasted an awful lot of time.

"You may think I'm happy, but I'm not," she finally told him one day. "This is on my mind all the time." It's true, once this concern developed for Alyssa, she could think of little else. It was a constant stressor, a splinter causing continual pain.

When I hear words like that I know this couple is dealing with a Selfish Hot Spot.

Kevin is happy with the way things are. He wants Alyssa in his life, but he's afraid to make any big changes. His father died just a few months before he and Alyssa started dating, and it seems hard to be in love with someone his father never met. When he thinks about it, he feels sad. Also, his parents were divorced when he was young, and that was so hard. How does he know that won't happen to him? He never got a good explanation from his parents about what went wrong. He imagines they entered their marriage with hope. Somehow that thought depletes his own hope.

To make things worse, his best friend Stew, who got married right out of college, has been crashing on his couch. He and his wife are having trouble. That's pretty scary.

A few months ago, when Kevin's lease ran out, Alyssa assumed they would get a place together. But he isn't ready for that. He likes his own space. He likes being with Alyssa, but he also likes being alone. On the mornings they're apart, he sleeps late, eats in bed, and sometimes masturbates. He would never be able to do that if he and Alyssa lived together. She likes to get up and eat at the table. When he thinks about it, he's pretty happy with his life right now. Why take a chance and change everything?

"I'm sorry if I'm being selfish," Kevin said to Alyssa. "I want you in my life, never doubt that, but I'm afraid to take a big step right now. I like my life the way it is."

This is the Selfish Standoff. Alyssa wants more, has waited for more, and given up valuable time in her twenties. Kevin is happy, in no rush, and hesitant to change his life. The way she sees it, she has so much to gain and not much to lose. The way he sees it, he could lose a lot. This standoff keeps Kevin and Alyssa locked in disagreement and discontent.

So often people come into my office with stories like these, and what they want to do from the start is prove that their partner is wrong. Alyssa thinks she's right: it makes all the sense in the world to want these things and move forward in life. Kevin thinks he's right: there is nothing wrong with taking their time. But people want to place blame. People want me to say, "Of course, you're right."

These are what I call the Fault Lines.

"It's your fault."

"No, it's your fault."

So whose fault is it? This is something I will address in more detail in chapter 4, but keep it in mind as we go through the many examples of Selfish Hot Spots. Time and time again, each partner is looking to place blame on the other. There is no margin for understanding. What sort of *we* is that?

The More the Merrier?

Let's look at another Selfish Standoff forming around another Big-Ticket Item: expanding a family. Maeve and Simon have been married for three years. He has an eleven-year-old son who lives with his mother. The agreement they made when they got married was that they would not have children. Simon already had a son and wanted no more children. Maeve always wanted children, but she accepted this and agreed to it because she wanted to be with Simon. She reasoned that she was older anyway, and if she waited much longer, she might not have children or a husband.

Recently, Simon's son started having trouble in school and in the community where he lived with his mother. Simon and his ex-wife decided it would be best to have him come live with him. Maeve reluctantly agreed.

Now everything Maeve thought was settled has come unhinged. Simon's son Eli is sweet and charming, but he's completely unreachable for Maeve. He will not let her in, and every time Maeve reaches out to him, he resists. Once she spent the day making brownies. She knew from various conversations between Simon and Eli that he loved brownies. And yet when Maeve presented them to him, he simply said he wasn't hungry. Another time Eli was watching a movie in the den. Maeve sat next to him on the couch and started watching too. Eli immediately stiffened, then made an excuse about homework and left the room. To make things worse, Maeve sees Eli hugging Simon freely all the time. She feels like the odd woman out. More than anything now, she wants to have a baby of her own. When she told Simon, he said no.

"You are so selfish," she said to him. "How can you ask me to raise your son and not be willing to give me my own child?"

Maeve became remote. She stopped making dinners, stopped dressing up as she usually did, stopped trying with Eli. She spent more and more time alone in the bedroom.

Simon had been so clear with Maeve from the beginning! Why was she acting like this? They were depleted, overwhelmed, completely taken up. There was no room in their lives for a baby. He was so busy worrying about Eli, making sure his needs were met, and checking in with his ex-wife, the last thing he wanted was to have another child. But Maeve was drifting away, leaving him emotionally. He had to do something. Finally, he agreed to try to get pregnant. But he felt more and more stressed. He could not imagine having another child in his house, another child to take care of and worry about. He was going to get lost! He started to have chronic stomach pain that his doctor worried might be the beginning of an ulcer. This had happened to him before, when he got divorced. Whenever he internalizes his problems, they go to his stomach.

Who is being selfish here? Maeve and Simon want different things, but they want to be together. How can this be resolved? Someone has to give in. But who?

These Big-Ticket Items become complicated when you and your partner don't see eye to eye. And when you don't, and your need isn't being met, you interpret your partner's actions as being emotionally selfish. A selfish partner appears to be thoughtless, inconsiderate, and dismissive. This leads the other partner to feel a wide range of negative emotions, including being dissatisfied, resentful, misunderstood, rejected, abandoned, lonely, uncared for, unloved, blamed, criticized, attacked, betrayed, and hurt.

Alyssa felt powerless and disappointed. Kevin felt scared and pressured.

Maeve felt confused and helpless. Simon felt trapped.

Often, as in Maeve and Simon's case, one person becomes more overbearing and takes a stronger stand. Maeve gives Simon almost no choice. He sees her slipping away, and he doesn't want that to happen. He gives in, but at this point he is giving in out of helplessness. He doesn't want to. He becomes physically ill and, as most people would, resentful.

When Maeve didn't get what she wanted, her actions translated into depriving behavior. She stopped cooking and hanging out. She spent time alone and became emotionally stingy. That is typical behavior in a situation like this. Then Simon gave in, but because she forced his hand, his whole well-being—emotional and physical—suffered. The focus now is on the negative for both of them. Why can't they each see it the other's way?

Another thing to note in Maeve and Simon's Selfish Standoff is that things changed during the course of their marriage that made Maeve reconsider her initial agreement. She never would have guessed that Eli would live with them and then, through that, her desire to have her own child would become overwhelming. Things happen during the course of a relationship that sometimes make the agreements made early on unbearable for one person or the other. And, of course, so often people enter an agreement at the beginning of a relationship thinking that, in the end, it's not going to matter so much to the other person. Surely they will come around. Once they were married, Maeve may have thought, *Simon will want to have a baby with me. How could he not?*

Challenging Faith

A similar thing happened with Tess and Pablo. She was raised in a Jewish home, and he was raised in a Catholic home. When they were dating, she came to love many of his family's traditions. She found going to Mass to be soothing and, even if she thought about her own concerns and ideas while she was there, she found she felt refreshed afterward. She also grew to love the holidays, the festiveness of Christmas and Easter. When they decided to get married, it was easy for her to agree to a Catholic wedding. When Pablo's mother asked her moments before she walked down the aisle if she planned to raise the kids Catholic, how could she say anything but yes? She was in a beautiful church, the organ was playing in the background, she loved Pablo so much!

When Celia was born, they didn't even discuss it. She was baptized. Two years later, Piper was born and she, too, was baptized. When Celia was three and Piper was one, Tess's older sister died suddenly. They immediately flew home to Boston to be with her family where all the usual Jewish traditions were under way. The funeral was planned for two days later—much faster than a Catholic funeral would happen. When they arrived home that evening, the house was crowded with people who were there to sit shiva, comfort the family, and pay their respects to the person who died. Tess took comfort in knowing people would be there every night for seven nights, as was the tradition.

Over the course of her week, Tess realized how much she missed being Jewish. She found great comfort in the words and the prayers. Did she really, when she got right down to it, have the same beliefs that Catholic people did? She didn't think so. When they got home a week later, Tess told Pablo she thought she had made a mistake. She wanted the girls to know what being Jewish meant too. Pablo went crazy, yelling that she had broken their agreement. How could she do that to him?

Pablo took a deep breath and told himself that Tess was upset because her sister had just died. She would come to her senses. But for weeks after she talked about it. One Friday night he came home to find the table set, candles in candlesticks, and a challah on the table covered with a cloth with Hebrew writing on it. What was going on? He felt enraged. But he went along with it, respectfully following Tess's lead. He hadn't even realized she knew the prayers! But the next day he said never again. His girls were Catholic. There was no question about it. He did not want to hear another Hebrew word spoken in their house, ever.

How will they get through this? Tess feels like she gave up so much and realized, after the death of her sister, that her childhood religion gave her great comfort. She was starting to feel so angry toward Pablo, why couldn't he be more open-minded? But Pablo, who was quickly losing respect for Tess because she was not holding up her end of the bargain, was not going to budge. His girls had been baptized, and they were going to Sunday school. Tess could take her Shabbat dinner somewhere else.

They were in the middle of the Never-Ending Fight—the vehicle that keeps whatever your Selfish Hot Spot is active and eruptive, like a volcano. Sometimes it's dormant, but you never know when the lava will erupt and bring the Hot Spot to life by creating turmoil and negativity. Whatever the disagreement is, it comes up either all the time or never, depending on your communication style. When it does surface, it always creates a combative climate of conflict and is the source of unhappiness for both of you. You and your partner find yourselves thinking, *I just can't get through to them. I just can't win.* You both end up feeling defeated.

With Tess and Pablo, each partner's different talking style only adds to the conflict. Tess wants to talk about it all the time. She imagines that if Pablo will just listen, he'll come around. Pablo thinks it will just go away, that once Tess has a little time to gain perspective, she will come to her senses. These different styles of communication only serve to compound the problem. Before they knew it, they were barely being nice to each other, stopped kissing good-bye in the morning, and hadn't had sex in weeks. She can't even think about having sex. She's lost respect for him, and the thought of sex is unimaginable. She wonders how she can be with a man who behaves this way.

At this point, when there is no clear way to turn, one person might play the Deal Breaker Card—that one thing that will send the other into a panic and will, most likely, force their hand. I want out. I want a divorce. I'm going to take the kids and go to my mother's. As Simon did with Maeve when he felt her moving away from him, this is when people will give in because they see no other choice. But it made Simon sick. So is Maeve really winning?

Paper Cuts

Now let's look at the Paper Cuts, the not-so-big-ticket items that can cause just as much damage. While the big issues are often more glaring and in your face, it's actually the smaller issues that can cause the most damage. These Paper Cuts are so surprising, often seeming to come out of nowhere, that they can cause complete chaos.

They are the things that drive you crazy about your partner that seriously compromise the quality of daily living, because they cut into your desire to please your partner. Instead of feeling loving and wanting to make your partner happy and comfortable, you're angry and holding on to a lot of resentment because of their actions. You can become consumed by these actions, and they become heavy clouds looming over you. Whatever your Paper Cuts might be, they are always bugging you or your partner, they are a constant irritant that ultimately translate into power struggles and control issues and leave you both feeling perpetually disappointed.

These power struggles basically boil down to a clash in needs (he likes to sleep with the fan on, but she doesn't). They're Selfish Hot Spots, and someone is bound to not get what they want. So how do you decide whose needs are more important? And—this is what confuses most couples—when do you compromise and when do you stand strong on an issue? How do you go about doing it?

Excuse Me, But...

One of the most common examples of these Selfish Hot Spots is interrupting or butting into another person's conversation. One partner will not let the other finish a sentence. He is constantly saying, "I can't get a word in edgewise!" It is a seemingly small thing, yet it has huge consequences. I have talked to couples many times in my office who have the same story. They spend a night out with friends, and when they get home, one or the other is livid. "You interrupted me the entire night! Every time I tried to say something or tell a story, you jumped in." The other person, however, is shocked. What is he talking about? I didn't interrupt him. We were just having a normal conversation.

A few years ago, I counseled Nina and Geoff. Nina would constantly interrupt Geoff. During our sessions, when she would cut him off, he would storm out of the room, furious and frustrated. He didn't have the tools to handle his anger effectively and point out to her (1) when she was cutting him off and (2) how it made him feel. Consequently, when he would walk out on her, she would throw up *her* arms in frustration and say, "See? We can't ever even have a simple conversation. He won't ever listen to me." Each partner is wounded by the other's behavior and feels as though they have been wronged. It's hard to weed through the mess and get to the root of the problem—whose selfish behavior started it? And if each person feels that their partner is being more selfish, how do you begin to solve the problem?

Conversation isn't the only thing that can be interrupted. One partner wants to hang out together while the other has important work to do. One wants to be quiet and enjoy the game, while the other wants to talk all the time.

Let's look at Brooke and Spencer. He hates being interrupted when he is engaged in an activity, any activity—paying the bills, raking the leaves, updating his iTunes library, watching a baseball game—but Brooke doesn't get that. When she wants to talk to him, she doesn't ever consider what he is doing. She will just talk at him. And when he doesn't stop what he's doing to answer her question or fulfill her request, she gets angry. "What's the big deal?" she always asks. She needs answers. What should she buy at the market for dinner that night? Can he take the kids for a few hours on Sunday? What does he think his mother will want for her birthday? And she needs answers now. Spencer is annoyed. He's saying, "You have to respect that I don't want to drop everything the minute you ask. Why must you always butt in on whatever I'm doing?" And Brooke is saying, "Stop what you're doing and pay attention to me! Can't you look at me when I'm talking? You are so rude. What could possibly be more interesting than me?" She feels unimportant and dismissed.

When they came into my office, Spencer asked why Brooke couldn't just wait until he was finished doing whatever he was doing. Brooke countered with the fact that she thought he was never finished. He took his time or moved immediately on to the next activity. Again, for each of them, it comes down to whose needs are more important?

This particular Selfish Hot Spot can morph into the ever-troubling *me* versus *we* time, when one person's need for individual time clashes with the other person's need to be together. Take Violet and Trent. He works ninety hours a week at his law firm. When he comes home, he wants to relax and play Guitar Hero to decompress from his day. Violet used to work with Trent at the law firm, but now she's home all day with the kids. She wants to spend her evenings with Trent, talking about their days or snuggling on the couch together. When Trent is holed up in front of the television with his game controller, Violet feels rejected, neglected, and unloved. But when she tells Trent this, he gets angry and often says, "Can't you just leave me alone for thirty minutes to unwind? I've been talking to people all day at work, and I'm tired." Violet's frustrated by his behavior. She doesn't understand. If he loved her, wouldn't he want to spend time with her? She believes he obviously cares about his game more than he cares about her, and it makes her hurt, angry, and question how she could be married to someone so uncaring. Why is he so selfish? Is she unreasonable in expecting him to sit and spend time with her? Is it realistic to expect him to give up his decompressing time? Is it unreasonable of him to expect her to understand that he needs time to himself?

The Stress Mess

What about the "I Am Way More Stressed than You Are" Selfish Hot Spot? Does it sound familiar? You think not only are you overworked and overburdened, but all the extra slack falls to you. Your partner would disagree. You couldn't possibly work harder than she does. You think taking out the trash is hard? Try taking care of the kids, proofreading medical journals all day on deadline, keeping the house stocked with food, cooking, and taking care of the family's three bulldogs.

Tabitha and Levi each think they are doing more than the other. There is no question about it. And each feels taken advantage of and burdened. I call this the "No Fair" Paper Cut. They are both professors at a local university and carry full course loads as well as advise a number of graduate students. They also have two boys, ages seven and nine, who have soccer games and piano lessons and karate classes. They are constantly arguing about being more burdened than the other. Typically, their days will be full of classes, meetings with students, taking one boy or the other to a class or a lesson, thinking about the next day's lessons, deciding what to have for dinner, and arguing over who will shop and who will cook. And after dinner is over, they still face hours of more work. But Levi has no problem stopping at a certain point. If the dishes don't get washed or the garbage sits for one more day in the cans in the garage, what difference does it make? But Tabitha can't stand it. She can't go to sleep until each item is checked off her list. As she runs around, Levi will often sit on the couch and play games on his iPhone. She screams at him to read to the boys or gather the newspapers for the recycling truck or get the school lunches together for the morning. He yells back that he won't. He has been working all day and will start the same cycle again in less than twelve hours. He needs to rest!

When a pipe bursts one night, flooding water into the downstairs powder room, Levi leaves it to Tabitha to clean up the mess and deal with the plumbers. For the twentieth time this year she feels that the unanticipated burden falls on her—staying home with a sick child, having to wait for a repair person, cleaning out the refrigerator after a power outage. And she would argue that the anticipated burdens also fall on her. If Levi cooks dinner twice a week, she cooks it the other five. He counters that he more than does his fair share around the house. He has a heavier course load since he's a tenured professor; she teaches three classes to his four. He would be happy to break that difference in hours spent teaching down for anyone who might ask. Usually she reluctantly accepts this argument. But now she is too far gone; she can't think straight. Why should she have to do it? She is at least as busy as he is. Their Selfish Hot Spot is quickly turning into an active volcano, and this is not unusual. Everyone feels that the balance of the scale is uneven. Each person feels they do more in the relationship, and that leads to feelings of being taken advantage of and being unappreciated.

This is particularly hard for Fran and Clark, although what they are dealing with is a bit different. I call theirs the "I'll See Your Stress and Raise You" Paper Cut in which neither person listens to or sympathizes with the other, leaving each feeling unsupported and misunderstood.

Fran is an advertising executive, having slowly moved up in the company for years, and it just so happened that shortly after they had their second child, she got the account she had been waiting for: a huge, expanding farm-to -table restaurant chain that was becoming increasingly popular. Clark, a journalist, has been working around the clock, covering corruption in their local city government. He is just about to break what he thinks is going to be the biggest story of his career. But it takes time and patience, and he is meeting with sources at all times of the day and night.

After work, Fran runs to the day-care center to pick up the girls and gets home just a touch after the kids should be eating their dinner. There's been no time to shop or even think about what to cook. The kids are cranky, Fran has a big presentation in two days, and she has not even had a second to go to the dry cleaner. The minute Clark comes in the door, she is talking at him.

"I had the hardest day ever," she says instead of saying hello. "I had back-to-back meetings from nine until six, and I had to leave before the last one was over. When I got to the day-care center, they were mad that I was late and charged me twenty-five dollars! Sydney was crying and Blakely was half asleep—I hope she isn't getting sick. We have nothing to eat, and I have to get that gray dress from the cleaner's sometime between now and tomorrow night."

Clark is still taking off his coat and tie. He comes into the kitchen where she is waiting for him to perform some miracle: be nice, suggest they order pizza, tell her that he will run out this minute to get her dress.

"You think you had a hard day!" he says with a not-all-together-kind look on his face. "There is no way it compared to mine. I spent most of it in the basement of city hall waiting for that employee I told you about to slip me a piece of paper that would prove the mayor has been doing what I know he's been doing. But without the paper, my editor won't run the story. I didn't eat lunch. The employee never showed. In fact, I think I might have to go back tonight…"

They aren't listening to each other. They are competing rather than relating. "You think you had a bad day? Well, let me tell you about mine…" Neither partner is willing to budge or acknowledge the other's stressful day. One stress-filled monologue is simply countered with another.

I Meant To!

Another common behavior that can drive a wedge between couples is forgetfulness. Did you make the doctor's appointment? Pick up bananas at the grocery? Mail in the check for the electric bill? If you've asked your partner to do something, and they forget to do it, it's hard not to take it personally, especially if the action meant a great deal to you. More often than not, your partner is so overwhelmed and caught up in their own life that they forgot about you. That's part of the problem. And indeed it's a selfish behavior that feels very personal, but it's *not about you.*

His forgetful behavior usually isn't deliberate. And even when there is an underlying subconscious motive of hostility and anger, it still isn't operating on a conscious, intentional level. In other words, even if forgetful behavior is coming from a place of anger, the person who is forgetting is likely out of touch with his anger. He doesn't consciously think, "I'm going to deliberately forget our anniversary just to upset her." Yes, the inaction is very upsetting, but it really is about their limitations and the difficulty they experience being in a relationship and having to consider somebody other than themselves.

Other actions include leaving dirty dishes in the sink, insisting on keeping the house at a certain temperature despite what makes your partner comfortable, an inability to be on time, different driving styles (I like to call this one "You're driving me crazy"), cooking styles that could include everything from salt preference (that is way too salty!) to one person's belief that you should clean as you go while the other person leaves it all for the end (I call this one "Cooking up a storm"), not showing enough affection, or showing too much affection. The list could go on and on.

I know these examples seem innocuous, but they are the core of the Selfish Game. They are the tiny selfish behaviors that are the underlying tremors in a relationship that eventually cause a huge earthquake. We have to get to the root of each selfish behavior, because once you understand why your partner is acting a certain way, it gives you the ability to handle it and respond in a positive manner.

Think of your last argument with your partner. What were you really fighting about? Was it about the fact that he never cleans the kitchen? Or was it how his never cleaning the kitchen makes you *feel?*

Leave It Alone!

Sometimes it's an outside source that causes the trouble in a marriage. For Marcie and Josh, it's his BlackBerry. In these economically challenged times, Josh has been even more stressed and attached to his office. It seems to Marcie that even when the two do manage to carve some time together, Josh is always on his BlackBerry, checking stocks or emailing clients. Marcie has come to resent that little piece of technology. She screams at Josh to put it down "for five whole minutes!" She doesn't understand why he can't step away from the BlackBerry while he's at home to show her that she is more important than work. Josh doesn't understand why she can't see that if he misses an important call or email, his career could go down in flames. So who's being more selfish? Whose needs are more important?

Marcie expects Josh to want to spend time with her more than his BlackBerry. She is begging him to pay attention to her. Josh expects Marcie to understand how important it is for him to focus on his career, especially now. Their difference in expectations results in serious miscommunication, taking the form of anger, resentment, and yelling.

Both Marcie and Josh are jockeying to put themselves first in the relationship in order to feel loved by the other and to feel good about themselves. Their behavior is a clear attempt to regain self-esteem. It's a power struggle that nobody gives in to. It's a Selfish Standoff that, if it doesn't get resolved, can break down the system. It's like the small leak in a yacht. Over time it's going to sink the boat.

And it doesn't have to be a BlackBerry that gets in the way. For Violet and Trent it's Guitar Hero. Or it can be the television, a video game, an obsessive need to wash the car. One person wants to be left alone to watch or play or scrub; the other wants to talk about the kids, about plans, about their relationship. Whatever. One person is saying, "Just let me be." The other is saying, "Pay attention to me." The same question must be asked, whose needs are more important? She doesn't feel special. He doesn't feel like he's being given the free time he deserves after working so hard.

Again, the Never-Ending Fight. You're always out with your friends, you drink too much, you never say I love you, you never do the laundry, how could you not want to have a baby with me. It's the one Selfish Hot Spot between two people that they try to avoid, but when it comes up, it can really bring down the house.

The big question is, Why is it so hard to reach a resolution? The answer: each partner takes the other partner's actions very personally. Maeve believes with conviction that if Simon won't have a baby with her, he must not love her the way she thought he did. On the flip side, Simon wonders if he's going to be able to trust Maeve as he always did, now that she's broken their agreement. He thought he'd married the most honest and loyal person he knew. Now, he isn't so sure. Similarly, Tess thought Pablo and she had an amazing exchange of ideas and positive emotions constantly flowing in their relationship. Why did Pablo suddenly turn on her? Pablo thought they had everything settled. The girls would be raised Catholic. How could Tess go back on their agreement?

For Alyssa and Kevin the issue is about commitment and moving forward. Alyssa is continuously eager to take the next step, but Kevin wants to take his time. How can they determine who will have the final say? Who will make the call on these decisions? If you asked any of the couples in my office, they would tell you that this isn't what they signed up for. This isn't what they expected from their partner. These Selfish Hot Spots, the ones they've been chewing on now for weeks and months to the point where they are raw and bleeding, just won't go away. If they want to save their marriages and relationships, the Selfish Hot Spots have to disappear. I can help. But we aren't quite there yet. Stay with me while these couples tackle the issues, and we strive to discover what is missing for each person and therefore causing the negative behavior. Some things are going to get worse before they get better. This negative energy almost always carries over to the bedroom, as we'll see in the next chapter about Selfish Sex. However, there are answers around the corner. These issues will have resolutions, and we'll find them together. But first, let's open those closed doors and see what's happening—or not—in bed.

Chapter 4

It's Always about You

Selfish Sex

LYDIA KNEW SHE HAD BEEN A LITTLE HARD ON JAKE LATELY, but she almost couldn't help herself. She was so exhausted she simply couldn't muster the energy to do anything about it, let alone care. Now, though, since she hadn't traveled at all this week and felt a bit better rested, she had a plan in place. She would cook a romantic dinner—complete with Jake's favorite pork tenderloin and some good wine—and maybe, just maybe she could somehow ease herself into the mood for sex. She even found the lilac nightie that Jake liked so much, just in case.

But that was hours ago. Forget about the nightie. Now she was in bed wearing her thick flannel pajamas and reading *The Ex-Wives Club*. This was what she usually wanted to do most, but tonight she couldn't get comfortable. She was so agitated.

Earlier, after she made the apricot glaze from scratch—she didn't want to use the store-bought apricot jam because she wanted this dinner to be special—she chose two bottles of wine and brought out the apricot-colored candles she had found that morning. The roast was carved and on the table, the candles were on their way to burning down, and Lydia had already had two glasses of the white when it occurred to her that Jake was not coming home for dinner. When he did finally call a bit later, he acted like it was no big deal!

Now Lydia hears the door open and she tenses. She listens as Jake goes through the house, turning off the lights and setting the alarm. He goes to the bathroom. She hears the water running. And then he's there, in the doorway.

"Hi," he says.

"Hi," she says back, not looking up from her book.

Jake had a great time at the hockey game. He knew she was mad based on her tone when he called, but he figured she would get over it; she usually did. Certainly, he guessed, if she had enough energy to cook dinner, she must have enough energy to have sex. All that excitement at the game really got his blood going. He isn't tired at all. He hesitates, and then climbs into bed. She is looking at her book, but he can tell she isn't reading. Sex would do them both a little good.

When she feels his hand creeping toward her, she figures she must be wrong. He wouldn't dare try for sex now. But there's his warm hand on her thigh and moving up toward the waistband of her pajamas. She turns to glare at him, grabs his hand, and lets out a sound that is a little like a cat's hiss.

"Are you kidding?" she asks through gritted teeth.

"What?" he asks.

"First of all, you knew full well that I planned to cook dinner tonight, because I told you this morning!" she says, her voice getting louder and louder. "And then you totally ignored that and chose to go out with your friend. But wait, there's more! You didn't bother to call me until I had already completed the task of cooking and getting the table ready, so I ate alone. And then I cleaned up alone. And now you expect me to have sex with you?"

Does this sound familiar? Can you see them, each layer of anger building on the next like an onion? The layers grow and form and smother your intimacy and, so often, dash your desire. And just like an onion can bring tears to your eyes when you slice it, attempting to dismantle the layers of your anger can cause sadness, pain, and emotional distress. But people are usually dumfounded by the other person's behavior, and they usually can't begin to recognize the layers. All they know is that they feel rejected and see the other person as acting selfishly. They don't have an understanding of the other's actions. Lydia thinks, *What about me? I went to all the effort to make a romantic dinner to put us both in the mood, and you don't even come home!* Jake thinks, *Are you kidding me? You have enough energy to read recipes and cook for hours, but you don't have enough energy to make love to me? And now, once again, you are going to say no to sex?*

Help me peel back Lydia and Jake's layers. It's not so hard to do when they have nothing to do with you. First, the makeup mirror, followed by Jake's anger and Lydia's not understanding it and making no attempt to change it, then his withholding tenderness and foreplay, her refusing to have sex with him, his deciding he wanted to skip dinner and go out with a friend, and her shutting down his sexual advances. Anger is layered with disappointment, which is layered with the instinct to prove each is in the right over and over again. Two things are happening: energy is depleted and desire is lost, but also, each is trying to protect themselves. That pipeline of resentment becomes constant. Where is this going to go?

For Lydia and Jake, their Selfish Hot Spot has led directly to this Sexual Showdown in which neither will give in, and consequently this has caused their sex life to come to a grinding halt. Each thinks, *What about me?* If all of your energy is being drawn toward a Selfish Hot Spot—fighting about the mirror or what temperature to set the thermostat or competing over who is more stressed out—then there isn't going to be much energy left over for your sex life. If 80 percent of your resources are consumed by anger—way more than half of what you have to offer to your partner—there isn't going to be much in reserve. Not to mention that when you're angry, it's hard to feel turned on. Again, desire is dashed—the shift going from wanting nothing more than to please your partner to its becoming the last thing in the world you would want to do. You move from always asking when can we do it, to doing it when you can if you can, to (in Lydia and Jake's case) not doing it at all.

Often this negative behavior, especially when it comes to Selfish Sex, seems to come out of the blue, and the partner on the receiving end is taken off guard. Jake was surprised when Lydia thwarted his advances, and Lydia was tremendously disappointed when Jake didn't jump onboard when she decided that the romantic dinner was just what they needed to get back on track. In these cases, the partner who is surprised is going to have to look at what their behavior might be contributing to the couple's interaction and thereby moving the other partner to either lash out or close down. More often than not, the seemingly out-of-the-blue unloving behavior can be traced back to emotional trouble. In other words, you just might discover that your actions have more to do with what is going on than you realize.

First, though, let's consider all the places things can go wrong in the bedroom and how people so often clash. Just as no two people have the same exact needs surrounding everyday issues as simple as driving or how to communicate, it is unlikely that those two people will have the same needs and desires surrounding sex, no matter how much you believed you did and would when your relationship began. When it comes to problems in the bedroom, I think of picket fences. Choose which picket to get stuck on. There are so many, but all it takes is one. Not only can it cause one or both partners to be consumed by anguish and despair, it can also bring your sex life to a grinding halt.

When this happens it affects what I call your Sexual Esteem, which is crucial to your healthy self-esteem. It can cut you to the core when you are not made to feel attractive or desired or good enough, because it is such an important part of your identity. It is a measure of your self-worth, and much like self-esteem, everyone is vulnerable to the approval and acceptance of their significant other. Both men and women look to their partner to reaffirm and assure them that they are sexy and their body is a turn-on. It doesn't take much to diminish your Sexual Esteem. Something as simple as your partner's not being in the mood or having a headache or taking a long time to come to bed can be perceived as a personal rejection and a blow to your sexual ego. You end up asking, What's wrong with me? What's wrong with you?

What are some of these common differences that people face in the bedroom? I've heard it all, from kissing to condoms. One couple can't agree on how much to kiss. She wants to all the time. He doesn't. Another couple can't agree on birth control. The woman refuses to put hormones into her body, but the man hates using condoms. What happens when one partner loves oral sex and the other doesn't? One wants to have sex three times a week, but the other thinks that is way too often. One likes to have sex every morning, but the other feels most turned on at night. Another wants to try new positions all the time, but her husband isn't much of an experimenter and likes to keep things simple. Issues around initiating sex, frequency, time of day, technique, and taste and preference generate so much fire for couples that there is often no heat left between the sheets.

Do YOU Think I'm Sexy?

Initiating—with a capital *I*—hangs over much of the sexual experience. Who initiates? How often? Who stops initiating (for whatever reason)? Over and over again in the years I've been in practice, one of the moments that comes up repeatedly and leaves people feeling insecure, unloved, and so many other negative emotions is waiting for sex to happen. The partner who is waiting hopefully wonders when their partner will initiate sex. There is a period of anguish for them, wondering when their partner is going to put the book down and turn to them. Is she ever going to come to bed? And when it doesn't go the way they hope, that partner experiences great despair from the sexual disconnect.

This became a major sticking point for Crystal and Allen. She loved having sex with her husband once they got going, but she found the waiting and wondering to be interminable. It was the endless wait, like waiting for Godot. Recently she told me of a night that was typical for them. They had dinner, cleaned up, and then, before Allen went into the den where his computer awaited, she walked over to him, hugged him, and very subtly thrust her pelvis toward him with what she described as a flirty smile. How could he not get that?

"I'm going to bed," she said, looking over her shoulder. He nodded and watched her go, smiling back. *Good,* she thought, *clearly he got the hint.* She took her time in the bathroom, debated what to wear, and decided nothing would be best. She got into bed and waited, at first smiling up at the ceiling and thinking over and over that she heard him coming toward her. Finally, she sat up a bit, wondering what he was doing. In her mind she had made it so clear. What could be more important than making love? Anything that he chose to do at that moment was in direct competition to her, as far as she was concerned. But no, that night was going to be different. She settled back down, gently touching herself a little in anticipation of Allen's touch. But then she heard his phone ring, and he answered it! He was still in the den! She could imagine him there, tapping away on his computer, checking a score or reading up on the latest breaking news. She pushed back the covers and found an ugly old T-shirt to pull on. She felt rejected, ugly, fat, not good enough. As those minutes passed while Allen finished his phone conversation, or set the alarm and went about the house to make sure everything was in order—occasionally getting distracted by a magazine article he had been meaning to get to—Crystal would lie in bed and think he didn't want to have sex with her.

"I don't feel loved or sexy or special or anything," she told me.

But unbeknownst to her, Allen did get the hint. He was thrilled by the prospect of sex that night. It was tempting to simply follow her into the bedroom, but he figured she wanted to take her time in the bathroom and then read a little. That's what she was usually doing when he got there. Besides, he was waiting for a call about a golf outing that weekend, he had some email to answer, and he liked things to be done before he retired for the night. The few times he went to bed early with the idea that he would get up again, he never did, and he would wake up in the morning to a computer still on, tons of unanswered emails, and a general mess. Better that he take his time now and then relax with Crystal later. Otherwise, he would be thinking about what needed to get done the entire time they were making love. He likes to feel free and then be able to drift off to sleep when they're finished.

When he got into bed, however, she had that ugly T-shirt on, and whatever he thought he had imagined from her was gone. She didn't even say hello or turn in his direction. Oh, well, maybe she wasn't in the mood tonight. He smiled, picked up his own book, and before he knew it, was ready to go to sleep.

The next morning she was still mad and stormed around.

"What's wrong?" he asked.

"I waited hours for you," she yelled. Her anger had been pent up all night. "It's your fault we didn't have sex once again. Are your phone and computer prettier than I am?"

"What are you talking about?" he asked, surprised. "It wasn't hours. It wasn't even an hour. Don't you know that I will eventually come to bed, but I just have to do what I have to do first?"

"You took so long! You always do. You don't have to read the newspaper or double check every window. I already did that! And if you leave a few emails until the next day, is that so bad?" she asked. "Is all of that more important to you than I am?"

There are a lot of different faces to initiating sex, and they are laden with very strong expectations that can lead to people feeling burdened and keeping score.

Tina and Jerome are dealing with this. He wants her to initiate sex every time. If you'll remember, he is a Taker and feels entitled. Not only does he want her to initiate sex, but he wants her to wait until he is ready—until the game is over or until he finishes talking to his brother on the phone. He figures if she initiates, then there will be no question that she is in the mood for sex. He doesn't want to waste his time if she is going to say no, but more than that, he is doing his best to avoid the disappointment he might feel, and he is protecting his Sexual Esteem from taking a hit should she reject him if he showed interest and she said no.

This doesn't work for Tina. Not only does she not want to always be the initiator, she also doesn't like waiting for him. So when she doesn't initiate, or when she gets mad when he spends two hours watching *Monday Night Football* instead of coming to bed as he said he would, he feels rejected and deprived. It is the ultimate illustration of the words, "But if you loved me, you would…"

Or what about Charlotte and Reed? She told him early on that she wants him to initiate sex between them, and she is enraged because he never does. He feels so much pressure that, to be perfectly honest, he is terrified he'll lose his erection. So he avoids it. She is so mad.

"I do everything around the house," she says to him. "I cook, I clean, I take care of the kids, I make sure the car is inspected on time. This is the one thing I ask of you, and you can't even do it?"

Whatever Turns You On...

There are other things people do on their way to sex that block the road. Role playing? Talking dirty? Heavy petting? Rough romance? What do you do when you don't agree on how to get from Point A to Point B? Or worse, what do you do when you are turned off by your partner's methods? One of my patients likes to talk baby talk to his wife before they make love. "Can we just snuggle wuggle?" he asks. But it makes her skin crawl. At first she could ignore it, and once they were actually having sex she was fine, but more and more lately his baby talk just kills her desire. Some women complain that, while they want their husbands to be gentle, instead their husbands will come up behind them, slap their butt, or grab them, and they feel instantly turned off. The husbands don't realize it; they think they are being playful.

Selfish Sex is when your partner wittingly or unwittingly puts their sexual preferences, needs, and desires ahead of your own, making you feel undesired, unattractive, and unloved. Like the mirror of romance, the mirror here is one of desire. Seeing our lover's passion for us in that mirror is crucial for our Sexual Esteem. This is all reinforced by our sexual intimacy, and when that isn't going well, when the mirror of desire turns into one of disgust, then you have bad feelings about yourself.

This is exactly what is happening with Lydia and Jake, and here is where it is going. Jake feels bad. They have not had sex for two months, which must say something about how much Lydia wants to be with him. But worse, the last four times he has decided to actually make an effort, she shut him down. Ouch. He's tired of initiating. He doesn't want to do it anymore. And Lydia, she's in bad shape. She had a great idea—she was going to bring some romance back into their lives with that dinner—she was making a huge effort to spice things up. And what did Jake do? He went out with a friend. Lydia has a bit more hope left in her than Jake does.

She decides she'll try to forget the dinner. Things are really tumbling downhill. Over the weekend they order pizza from their favorite local restaurant and enjoy it in front of a movie they've been meaning to watch. When it's over, with the pizza dishes still on the coffee table in front of them, she takes Jake's hand and kisses it. He lets her, but he isn't jumping in. She then moves his hand slowly down to her crotch. She's wearing a flowing brown linen skirt so it would be easy for him to touch her. Only her pretty yellow underwear stands between them.

But Jake has had it. Her last sexual rejection was the end of the road for him. He's tired of initiating, and worse, he wants her to know what it feels like to be rejected. So he pushes her hand away and stands, lifting the dishes one by one. He leaves her stunned on the couch.

The Selfish Package

This problem—this Selfish Hot Spot—was clearly brewing in their relationship before it made its way into their bedroom. But now that it's there, combined with the Sexual Showdown, it has become what I call a Selfish Package. They are packed in tightly between two smoldering Hot Spots with no place to go. They are losing each other. The emotional negativity turned into sexual negativity, and the bread on both sides is getting thicker, with fewer air holes, and their relationship is trapped in the middle.

So what happened to that crazy, hot lovemaking in the broken chair in the kitchen while Jake did his laundry? How can their sex life take such a dark turn? It's scary to think people can start out like Lydia and Jake and end up someplace completely different. So often at the beginning of a relationship, two people want to make love all the time, but it almost never holds at that high level.

Remember in *Annie Hall* when we see Woody Allen's character saying to his therapist that his lover never wants to do it, maybe twice a week. And then the screen flashes to Diane Keaton's character, talking to her own therapist, saying he wants to do it constantly, at least twice a week!

Let's consider Jenna and Gabe. She was happy to have sex once a week or so, usually on a weekend when they weren't both stressed from their jobs and busy days. But that wasn't good enough for Gabe. Do you recall how he wanted to force Jenna to commit to having sex a certain number of times each week if he agreed to have a baby? And how Jenna refused to move to Texas to be with his family? He throws that back in her face all the time. He wants to have sex three or four times a week, surprising her when she is certain they are resting for the night. She works hard, her feet ache, she is so happy to lie down. The lights will be out, she will be settling into the mattress, starting to drift off, and she'll feel his hand at her vagina, pushing its way in.

When she says no, he gets angry.

"You made me stay here when I want to be in Texas," he often says. "This is the least you can do. You are a terrible wife. Look at everything I've done for you, everything I've given up for you. And this is how you treat me?"

Often he'll tell her that he makes most of the money, it is his job that allows them to live in this nice house and go on all the nice vacations, so basically she owes him.

"I can't believe you are bringing all these things up again," she finds herself saying again and again. "It is so unfair. I wish you would stop making me feel guilty. Can't you see how tired I am?"

The problem is, she simply doesn't have the sex drive to keep up with his desire. Not to mention that his anger and guilt-inducing coercion are a turn-off. Her desire has been further compromised, and she is cut off from her own Sexual Esteem. He is a Controller—in all aspects of their lives. In this case, it is translating into being a sexual bully.

By the time she came to my office, Jenna was consumed with guilt and was trying to figure out what she was doing wrong. She also asked, "Do I have to have sex with him?" She said his overactive sex drive makes her feel like an object.

The more Jenna held off, the angrier Gabe got. He didn't get it. She agreed to marry him. She certainly knew he liked to have sex regularly. Isn't that part of what she agreed to, even wanted? And, really, he doesn't ask for it so often. If it was up to him, he would do it every day. So three or four times a week is a good compromise, right?

Timing Is Everything

Let's take a peek at Loretta and Sid in the bedroom. They both want to make love and share intimacy, but as far as Loretta is concerned, Sid is too quick and there is absolutely no foreplay involved. Time and time again she has no opportunity to get turned on, not to mention actually feel satisfied. She can barely get her clothes off before he is done. No matter how many times she says she would like a little foreplay, or gently guides his hand to her breast, he is right on to the next thing. But Loretta is a Martyr, and even though his sexual technique is miserable as far as she is concerned, she doesn't want to risk telling him for fear of upsetting him or making him angry. The very few times she dared mention anything in the past, he blew up and she felt terribly guilty. So she suffers silently. She thinks it is her responsibility to keep him happy, even at the cost of her own pleasure.

But she thinks about it—all the time. Last night she told herself she would slow him down. But she honestly couldn't. She tried to caress his penis for a while, thinking maybe that would prolong the sex and give her a chance to get in the mood. Maybe he would even touch her a little. Boy, was she wrong. He got so excited so fast that he threw her hand away and entered her aggressively. She found herself on her back, not at all ready for this, with her legs up in the air and her husband pumping away. She kept trying to tell herself to get in the moment, think about his penis in her vagina, maybe she could get in the mood. But then he was speeding up, pushing harder, not paying any attention at all to her attempts to slow him down. And then she felt them, his final thrusts, and she scolded herself for even trying. He sat back with a big smile and seemed perfectly happy. She stayed where she was, on her back with her legs still open, trying so hard to stop the tears from falling. They were burning in her eyes, but she didn't want to be one of those women who cries after sex. So she smiled weakly, folded her body together, and scooted to the bathroom, where she cried until she was sure Sid was asleep, and then she crept into bed quietly.

All Sid could think was that that was some of the best sex they had ever had. How could things keep getting better and better? He was a lucky man! She hadn't touched his penis in a while. He loved that! Now he was going to drift off to sleep with his lovely wife by his side.

When they first came to see me, Loretta felt so guilty. Her intense fear and anger about disappointing him made her go along with what she felt was Selfish Sex for so many years. She didn't see any choice. When I asked if she had told him how she felt, she said no. The few times she tried, he made her feel as guilty as ever.

Sid, of course, was clueless to her feelings. Because she didn't dare talk about it, he had no way of knowing she was so unhappy. So while Sid's behavior seems to be completely selfish to Loretta, it clearly was not intentional. He had no idea that she felt this way, and he was mortified when he found out. In his mind they were having great sex, because she let him believe that and it was always good for him.

Foreplay is often an issue. For the partner who wants it but isn't getting it, it is a tremendous loss. That's why communication about sexual needs and desires between couples is so important and yet so tricky. Maybe if Sid understood that Loretta needed more time, he would make an effort. But almost everyone is sensitive when it comes to their sexual prowess, so sometimes it can do more harm than good. The danger is that he might take her comments as criticism—most likely he fancies himself to be a great lover—and this perceived criticism could have a negative impact on their love life. She is afraid of running the risk of insulting him.

Just Tell Me What You Like...

One negative remark, even if it's said in the hope of change, can bring your sex life to a dead stop.

In fact this happened with my patients Risa and Wade.

"I wish you wouldn't be so sloppy when we're French kissing," Wade once said to Risa in a moment of honesty. He found her to be messy and have so much saliva that he just couldn't enjoy it. Do you know what happened? Risa didn't kiss him for twenty years because she was so wounded by it. She kept her mouth shut tight—literally and emotionally. And this affected their sexual encounters from there on out. She was afraid to put her whole self into it anymore for fear of being criticized. What if Wade thought she was doing it wrong? At any moment he might tell her he didn't like how she was touching him or that she was moving to what he thought was an incorrect rhythm. Her heart and soul stood on the sidelines when they made love after that.

When people are criticized, they feel a need to protect themselves. Negative communication can cause guilt, anxiety, or resentment, which can lead to someone's becoming sexually inhibited and afraid to try new things for fear of criticism or judgment from their partner. That, in turn, can easily lead to the kind of performance anxiety that debilitates sexual intimacy.

This is also true when it comes to having an orgasm—a common picket people get stuck on. One person might place great importance on the other person's having an orgasm. It might not even seem like successful sex to them if an orgasm isn't achieved by their partner. If you feel this pressure, that you have to climax no matter what, that there is no room for the possibility that sometimes you might not, then the groundwork is laid for faking it. And that is never good. This, of course, can also lead to performance anxiety, or pleasure anxiety, and it can debilitate sexual intimacy. So if you and your partner don't meet eye to eye on sexual needs, and you constantly butt heads about it—whether it is spoken or unspoken—you could end up avoiding sex altogether, which creates a huge disconnect in couples and compromises intimacy.

Let's peek in at Marcie and Josh. Remember them and his BlackBerry? Well, you can imagine if that BlackBerry carries so much weight and generates so much anger outside the bedroom, what it could do inside the bedroom.

Josh likes to have sex in the morning. He wakes up with an erection and is ready to go. But Marcie is a night gal. In the morning she is sleepy and feels messy. She likes to do it just before bed. To her, it is the perfect way to unwind after a busy day.

Recently she agreed to do it in the morning. They talked about it the night before, so she was ready and, she decided, she was going to do her best to enjoy it. She was still drowsy when he reached over for her, and it was kind of nice to move toward Josh with her eyes still closed, her dreams still in her head. She reached for his penis, which, as promised, was ready and waiting. She opened her eyes and smiled, leaning in to kiss his penis. She almost missed the sound of his groan because the ring of his BlackBerry was so jarring. It rang once, and he hesitated. She was hopeful, though, and wrapped her hands around his penis.

"Wait," he said, unbelievably. "I think this is about my morning meeting."

It was the last straw.

I'll Tell You What I Don't Like

Mary Beth and Neil have a problem. He loves getting blow jobs. They are probably the things he likes best in life. He dreams about them, fantasizes about them, and yet Mary Beth hates to give them. The bottom line is, she thinks they are yucky. She doesn't want to jam his penis into her mouth. On the rare occasions that she does, she is so tense, so terrified that he is going to come in her mouth without warning that she never gets turned on.

Every time they start to have sex, Mary Beth tries to keep their heads together. She kisses him and whispers in his ear. But inevitably she starts to feel his hand urging her head toward his penis. They don't talk about it at that moment, but she will usually refuse or redirect. Sometimes she'll stroke his penis and then guide it toward her. After they're finished, however, they have the same conversation again and again.

"Aren't you ever going to give me a blow job?" he asks.

"You know I don't like to," she says. "We had good sex without it, though, didn't we?"

"Well, sure, it was fine, but I want a blow job. Are you telling me that I am never again going to have a blow job? Why would you want to deprive me of one of life's great pleasures?"

"Are you telling me that you want me to do something I hate?"

"So you hate it?"

Make no mistake, this is not a male-female preference. It is a personal preference and has become a problem for Florence and Rafael too. She loves oral sex—to receive it and give it—always has. But he just doesn't get it. Quite frankly, it seems dirty to him. And yet he often feels he has to, but he doesn't enjoy it one bit. He thinks about how she peed from that spot just moments ago, and that it is not a place his face is supposed to be. Rafael likes the feeling of when she gives him oral sex, but he feels so guilty about not wanting to reciprocate with her that he can't relax. So every time she tries, he eases her away to avoid feeling bad.

Florence wants it so much. In fact, the best orgasms she has are during oral sex. She has a hard time climaxing during intercourse. When Rafael is just a little farther away from her, not looking right at her, doing whatever he does with his tongue, she can relax and be swept away. And she certainly doesn't mind doing it to Rafael. It's fun. But he rarely lets her. Rafael honestly doesn't know how he is going to get through a lifetime of doing this. He tenses and sometimes even loses his erection when she eases his head toward her vagina. Once he found a piece of toilet paper sticking there. Yuck! She knows he doesn't love it, but certainly he can stand it to give her pleasure, can't he? Whose needs and desires should win out? Again, "If you loved me, you would…" Or, in Rafael's case, "If you loved me, you wouldn't ask."

Gail and Henry are losing each other. It started to happen a while ago, depending on whom you ask, maybe as long as three years ago, when their fourth child was born. All she ever wants is to be with her two best friends, who happen to be their neighbors on either side of their city row house. So it is a little too easy to be together. Gail wants to do everything with them and their families: have dinner numerous times a week, go on weekend outings. It's fun, sure, but Henry longs to be alone with her and the kids. It's rare that he comes home to an empty house. More often than not he finds one or the other or, most likely, both of the neighbors and their kids filling his house. There is no time to talk about their days or make their own decisions. It drives him crazy.

You would think that the bedroom would be the one place they might find some alone time. But not lately. One of the neighbors told Gail that she thought it was awful to be on the pill indefinitely, so Gail stopped taking it. She refused to investigate other birth control options. Henry knew his sister used a diaphragm, but Gail wouldn't even consider it. So the only choice is to use condoms, which he truly hates. He would rather masturbate alone than use a condom. So that is what he started to do most mornings in the shower as his family clamors outside the door. Their conversations are always the same.

"I can't believe how selfish you are. Why can't you at least check into other possibilities of birth control. What about a diaphragm? There are lots of choices," he'll say. "You are so lazy. You would rather I don't enjoy sex than take time out of your day—away from the neighbors—to find a solution that works for both of us."

"So you want me to put chemicals into my body for your own pleasure?" she says back. "You might think I'm lazy, but let me tell you, I think you're selfish."

On the rare occasions Gail does want to have sex, he doesn't. He just masturbated hours before, and his sex drive is shot. Now, he realizes when he thinks about it, they haven't had sex in four months. He knows that isn't good, but he isn't sure how to get back to it. And he hates those stupid condoms.

Emily and Ned are also having a hard time finding each other, but it isn't their method of birth control. It is Ned's fashion choice, and it is leading them to the same place Henry and Gail are right now: nowhere in the bedroom. Emily is having a hard time mustering up the desire to sleep with Ned. Remember them from chapter 2? He lost his job and is struggling to get back on track, and she not only lost patience but also respect for him and, she fears, her attraction to him. For her, the obvious physical problem is that he wears the same stinky, ugly flannel shirt every day. When she asks him why, he says it's comfortable. He's so tired of wearing suits, he's happy to have a chance to wear what he wants. Besides, he says, what's the point of dressing up? He isn't seeing anyone he knows anyway.

But to be perfectly honest, she thinks he's being slovenly and finds the shirt to be repulsive. She imagines she can smell it from across the table. And what does he mean he isn't seeing anyone he knows? He's seeing her, isn't he? For her, that shirt has turned into a symbol of everything she doesn't like about what he's become. So when he reaches for her in bed, usually still wearing that shirt, she makes up some excuse and turns her back to him. She just can't help herself.

Initiating sex, foreplay, technique, frequency, birth control, underlying emotional Selfish Hot Spots—these are all issues that come up again and again and find their way into your bedroom. And when they show their ugly heads, the Fault Lines I first mentioned in chapter 3 come into play.

"You hurt me," one thinks and says.

"No, you hurt me," the other responds.

These Fault Lines—which are always hard to call—become almost impossible to decipher in the sexual arena. Who is hurting whom and who started it? A few miles down the road with this continued behavior, and you or your partner might shut down. Once you resign yourself to being unhappy in your relationship—in other words, when you move beyond your anger and give up on finding happiness in the intimacy you share with your partner—you usually disconnect from your desire both sexually and emotionally.

Lydia and Jake are traveling down that road. They are both exasperated and tired of trying, and each feels like the other clearly wronged them. They still have a bit of fight in them, but how long is that going to last—especially if they continue to perceive the other's actions as a direct insult? And this is where a marriage runs the risk of one partner becoming unfaithful. When you aren't getting what you need from your marriage, you start asking, Is there something wrong with me? And sometimes you look for external input to find the answer you want—that there isn't.

One partner might still think things are okay, because the other has stopped fighting, but in reality the other person may have given up and simply accepted all the negativity. If these issues aren't resolved in a way where both partners are satisfied, a disconnect begins like a crack in a windshield and will keep spidering out until the windshield (or relationship) is beyond repair.

The roles you determined yourselves to be in chapter 1 almost always carry over to the bedroom. And so often those roles might not serve you or your partner in the best way. Crystal is a Giver, but she feels rejected. Jerome is a Taker, and Gabe is a Controller, and they are both alienating their spouses. And Rafael is a Martyr, giving Florence oral sex to please her but hating every minute of it.

In addition to everything else that's going on in the bedroom, it comes down to this: in any sexual encounter there are two players—the sexual Taker and the sexual Giver—these roles can be expanded to include the extremes of the Martyr and the Controller. The Giver does most of the initiating, and the Taker reaps most of the benefits. In a perfect relationship, each person should be able to be both the Giver and the Taker. But as we've seen with many of these examples (and what may be happening in your bedroom) is that there is no fluidity between roles. You give and your husband takes. Or you demand and he reluctantly performs. The one who is pushing for sex is perceived as the sexual bully, while the one who is withholding is perceived as the sexual miser.

With the tools that we are now about to discuss, you will be able to not only learn to compromise about the Selfish Hot Spots, but you will also be better able to give and take in the bedroom. If only Gail could spend less time with the neighbors and more with Henry, then maybe he would be able to work with her to find a solution for birth control that would please everyone. If only Ned would take off that stupid shirt, get up off the couch, and in Emily's eyes, pull himself together. On the flip side, if only Emily could understand he was having a hard time and cut him a little slack. If only… If only…

These "if only" instances are like wallpaper in your bedroom—always there glaring at you—and you have to move beyond them and even erase them. Unfortunately, for so many couples, retaliation becomes their only means of communication. If you are like these people—trying to reach your partner through retaliation—then stick around. There might be hope around the corner, and it might be easier to find than you expect.

Part 2

Moving from Me to We

Chapter 5

Loving Me without Losing Us

Every time Jenna dared suggest anything—that they spend the weekend or even just an afternoon with her family, for example—Gabe would bring up Texas.

"We could be with my family now, hanging out with them. But we're not," he would say. "Spending time with your family would just rub it in. I don't want to."

On the rare occasions they did see Jenna's family, Gabe made her miserable. He would complain and ask constantly when they could leave. Or worse, when her parents were at their house, he would remove himself and work on his BlackBerry the whole time they were there.

He made her constantly feel guilty about the single thing in their marriage she stood up for—not moving to Texas to be with his family. Everything they did had to go his way because, in his mind, she had deprived him of such a big opportunity. He controlled the money and made all of their decisions: what to eat, where to shop, where to go on vacation, what charities to support, what color the front door of their house should be, whom they would spend time with. Some of this wasn't a surprise. Jenna knew Gabe was controlling before they got married. But she ended up feeling like she had to give in to him every time. This is what I call Guilting In—when you give in because you see no other way and doing so alleviates your guilt. It is not a genuine choice. In other words, you are motivated by your own guilt, not by a genuine desire to please your partner.

For the first few years Jenna came to see me, she did not tell Gabe she was going to therapy. But he eventually found out, and as you might imagine, he was not happy. He demanded that she stop. And here is where Jenna reluctantly made that first step toward reclaiming herself: she refused to stop coming to therapy. Now remember, the last time she stood up to Gabe, he never let her forget it. So this was a big deal for Jenna. I suggested she tell him it was doctor's orders so that it would take a bit of the responsibility off of her shoulders. We were already making progress, and this was the beginning of the turning point in Jenna's realization that she, too, had a right to be emotionally healthy and feel good. She was slowly learning to trust herself because she had begun to feel safer and more grounded.

Through therapy, Jenna was able to understand why she behaved the way she did and why she let Gabe walk all over her. When she was a child, her younger sister Rhea was ill. Rhea's heart was not fully formed when she was born, so she never received a proper amount of oxygen. She slept a lot, couldn't run or dance, and when she exerted herself—to demand a toy or something else—she got so tired it scared her mother terribly. Consequently, Jenna's parents always placed the emphasis on her sister. Rhea's needs came first. If Rhea wanted a toy that Jenna was playing with, even if it was Jenna's own toy, they forced her to hand it over before Rhea got upset. Also, if Rhea was sleeping, Jenna had to be completely quiet. If she was playing or laughing or having fun, her parents would almost always tell her to stop, because it upset Rhea in one way or another. Jenna constantly heard, "Stop that! It isn't fair to your sister. She isn't as lucky or as healthy as you are."

As a child, Jenna learned that she had to hide any fun she had. She hid in her room, sometimes even in her closet, and played her games or read her joke books, but she grew to connect those activities with feeling guilty. She always felt like she shouldn't be doing them. She associated being happy with doing something wrong. So she hid more and more, eventually, in essence, hiding from herself.

Focusing on her development as a child also helped Jenna understand that having fun did not have to be associated with guilt. She started to see that she had as much right to feel good and have fun as anybody did.

Understanding this helped Jenna begin to tackle the guilt she felt toward Gabe. She finally realized that the "Texas decision" was not her fault. She came to see that she had never agreed to move to Texas in the first place. Never. She had simply agreed to think about it, which she certainly had done. And after she was finished thinking about it, she realized that moving to Texas was not what she wanted to do. Knowing this helped her slowly stop feeling guilty about that major, recurring obstacle in their marriage and eased her toward being able to stand up for what she wanted.

Another problem Jenna had was her anxiety, and the therapy sessions helped her learn how to manage and reduce her panic attacks. Once she realized that, she was completely unwilling to stop coming to therapy, no matter how aggressively Gabe pushed her to. The combination of learning what was right for her and lessening her guilt helped her be strong when Gabe demanded things of her using his usual guilt tactic. Eventually, Gabe begrudgingly accepted her coming to therapy as well as the slow change in the dynamic of their relationship. He still fights her on both issues, but she is stronger now. She finally found relief and some safety and was willing to stand her ground in a way she was not able to before. Her own personal fears finally trumped her fears of his reaction to her. Jenna and Gabe are now on the road to fixing their marriage. And, Jenna is happy to note, they spend much more time with her family.

SelfNess

One of the most important things to remember while reading this chapter is that there is, beyond a shadow of a doubt, what I call healthy selfishness—which each partner in a relationship must achieve and maintain—and I call this SelfNess. Just as Jenna finally did, you have to cope with your guilt so it doesn't hold you back from experiencing joy and fulfillment in your life. You have a right to expect your partner to be responsive to you. You must come to be able to ask for what you want and need, especially for the things that feel vital to your well-being. It is also important to feel free to express your feelings and stop hiding how you really feel—your true self.

But before we try to understand SelfNess, we have to fully understand selflessness. Most of the Martyrs and Givers we've looked at and will continue to dissect in this chapter are lacking the SelfNess I am talking about. They operate from selflessness and have completely given up their own needs in an effort to make their relationships work.

If you fall into this category, then your identity comes from what you do and give to your partner; it has little to do with who you are and what you actually need. The qualities that make you who you are—your quirks, preferences, even your personality—get lost in the mix.

Because of what happened to Jenna when she was a child, she started to lose herself and what she wanted and needed because she hid from her family and ultimately from herself. When you hide like that you lose yourself. And before you know it, you've disappeared. If you disappear, then so do your needs and desires, and what's left in your relationship are only your partner's needs and desires. Fulfilling those are what you focus all of your efforts on.

Martyrs and Givers find their self-esteem not by making sure their own needs get met but by meeting the needs of their significant others. Their sense of self depends on what and how they give and do for their partners. And just like Jenna, this might have to do with what was missing emotionally from their child-hoods—whether it was a depressed mother, a sick sibling, a divorce, a drug-addicted family member, or an absentee father. When things like that happen, there is no time or energy left over to nurture children, so those children come to feel that they don't deserve good things in their lives and that somehow they are not good enough. When they become adults, they will often attach themselves to partners who know how to take advantage of that developmental quirk, and they will continue to believe that they never measure up, because they are now in another situation that presents a slew of unreachable and unappreciated demands.

There are other reasons why Martyrs and Givers give up on their needs. Sometimes they simply want to avoid the severe disappointment that comes their way when they dare voice their needs or desires and their partners say no. And over time, as they stop speaking up, they lose their voice. Now let's meet Veronica, Sadie, Claudia, and Maya, four Martyrs for whom selflessness was a way of life.

Veronica told me she didn't even let herself hope that her part-ner Reuben would do anything for her or go along with anything she asked for; that way she would never be let down. When they first got married, she would see advertisements for plays and mov-ies that she would have loved to see, but when she mentioned them to him, he always said he didn't want to go. And he wasn't particularly nice about it.

One week, she remembers, she asked him to go with her to see a movie that had gotten four stars in the newspaper. He said absolutely not, it was a Sunday, and on Sunday he always liked to take it easy and didn't want to leave the house. He made her feel bad that she even asked. Certainly she should know this about him.

That Tuesday she talked to a few co-workers who had seen the movie and said it was one of the best of the year. On Tuesday nights they tended to have casual dinners—pizza or sandwiches—so she thought it would be fun to go out for a few slices and then see the movie.

"Why are you always nagging me?" he asked harshly when she called him and excitedly presented her idea. "Drop it already, and stop pressuring me."

This became his standard line.

She gave up on the movie, but for their first year or so of marriage she kept trying. She suggested starting up a weekly card game with neighbors, getting season tickets to the orchestra, and going to a cabin in the country with friends. And every time Reuben said no. He called all the shots when it came to what they did for fun and how they spent their money in that regard. He always made time for his own friends, but never for hers. Finally, she stopped suggesting and asking. And then she stopped hoping.

Veronica, like Jenna, did not have a happy childhood, and some of this behavior can be traced back to that. When she was young, her parents fought constantly. Every time her family planned something that was supposed to be great fun, her parents would begin to argue, and it would escalate until either the outing was canceled or Veronica and her brother were in tears and completely unable to enjoy whatever they were doing. Once, she remembers clearly, they planned a holiday carriage ride through a park near their home. It was a big deal, with horse-drawn carriages and tickets bought in advance. All she remembers about that evening is her parents' fighting, her father's jumping out of the carriage while it was moving, and the driver's yelling at him. For a moment she thought maybe they could still have fun, now that her mother didn't have anyone to fight with. But her mother called to the driver to stop, and everyone got out and trudged through the cold night back to the gate she had entered with such hope and anticipation. She was so mad—mostly at herself. When would she ever learn? There are different sides of guilt being born here. For Jenna, whose sister was sick, all the oxygen was sucked out of the family, and there was none left to let her thrive. When she tried to take some for herself, she was taught to feel guilty. But for Veronica, her parents were always angry. Without fail, every time they tried to celebrate or go somewhere, it was ruined. Her own hope became her source of feeling bad.

Then and now, for Veronica, there came a need for self-protection. When she asked for her needs to be met she felt vulnerable—like she was putting herself out there to be struck down. Her husband got angry or annoyed and flat out rejected her ideas, and she felt sad with no way out. She loved him and wanted to be with him and please him. So her needs became his needs. Her whole purpose in life moved away from thinking about herself and moved toward being there to serve him. She completely stopped considering what she would like to do and see and thought only about what he would like to do and see. Even the way she read the movie reviews in the newspaper or heard about great deals on vacation homes changed. She thought about them with only him in mind now.

If any of this sounds familiar, it is possible that you didn't get enough individual attention or interest shown to you when you were a child. You may have learned that you have to sacrifice what is important to you—your toys, your time, your hope, your space—for the sake of whoever might need it more. This is the start of feeling good about yourself based on what you give up for the people around you. Having things for yourself becomes associated with guilt, and you see yourself as selfish and greedy if you ever want anything. But you can never give up enough or meet the demands that are made of you, and therefore you never develop a clear sense of self based on your own merit. Consequently you may feel inadequate and not good about yourself.

Martyrs and Givers give in all the time, although for some it is after putting up a fight. They might try to say no and stand up for what they want or need, but they often end up overpowered by the other person's angry reaction or their own guilt. They reach a point where it just doesn't seem worth it. Basically, they give up. They stop thinking about their own hopes and desires and what is important to them, and instead they think about what their partner wants and expects from them. They put themselves in their partner's head instead of staying in their own. This reinforces their feeling deprived and feeds into the need to do more for the other person. Their self-esteem is met by being the needed one. Doing for their partner becomes what makes them feel good. They preserve their value, security, and importance by feeling that their partner could not make it in the world without them. This perception of their partner's dependency on them relieves the fear that they will be abandoned since many of them may have felt abandoned in one way or another as a child. It is a vicious cycle: the less they get, the more they give; the more they give, the more their partner expects and, in turn, the less their partner gives.

This happened to Sadie. It was a slow process that took place over years, but she incrementally gave up pieces of herself to be there for her husband Jonathan. First, she stopped her weekly manicures, then her workouts at the gym, then the walks that she substituted for the gym became less and less frequent. She canceled her regular lunches with friends so many times they eventually stopped including her.

Jonathan was a contractor in the neighborhood, and he used their home as an office. So all his paperwork and supply overflow was in the house. Sadie would be about to go to the gym or go shopping or do some of her own work as a freelance software salesperson, when Jonathan would call and ask for help. "Can you bring me that box of screws on my desk? I'm just down the street." "Can you check that invoice to see what kind of knobs they want on their cabinets? Do you think you could drive quickly to Home Depot and pick those up?"

Sadie gave up the manicures first because she would be unable to help him while her nails were wet, and she felt anxious about that. Then she slowly stopped exercising, because it was a rare day she made it through her workout without hearing from him. And then, she realized, she hadn't read a book in months, because there was so much to do in the office. Her magazines were piled up unread next to her bed. Her days started to revolve around his business, and her nights had long revolved around his needs. What did he want for dinner? When did he want to have sex?

For Sadie, selflessness became the norm. She counted on the fact that Jonathan needed her so much. She came to depend on it for her self-esteem. It became the way she defined herself. Fulfilling his requests and demands made her feel important. But she was suffering. She put on weight and knew she looked terrible. She had no time to shop for new clothes to fit her bigger body, so she started wearing sweats all the time. She stopped doing freelance work, so she had no extra money that she felt was just hers. To be perfectly honest, she never even thought about what she wanted or what she was missing. Her needs were nowhere in this picture. The balance in their marriage was completely lopsided.

Jonathan, of course, was a Taker. He expected to be given to. And over time, he asked for more and more and more. And to make things worse, he usually framed his requests in such a way that it seemed like he was doing Sadie a favor to let her help him. Takers, like Jonathan, are skilled at turning things around and making it seem like you're lucky to help them. You don't even realize it's happening, and before you know it, you, like Sadie, are jumping through hoops.

Sadie was flattered that he deemed her as skilled, even though there was a part of her that knew he was just too lazy and cheap to hire someone to do what she did. He never suggested she become an official employee of his company, even though she was working so hard. When they were out with friends, and they would ask what she was up to lately, Jonathan would laugh and say she was his gofer. Jonathan's requests were indulgent and self-serving, but at the same time, he never for a minute thought Sadie wouldn't follow through with them.

Along the same lines, Claudia and Rick had finally decided to move in together. They had been dating for almost a year, and she loved being with him. Sure, he seemed to have an awful lot of needs. And she had noticed that he was still extremely close to his mother, who would drop anything to come to his rescue. And there was that fact that he was a doted-on only child. But she was confident that would all shake out. She wanted to be in a relationship with him, she was sure of that.

One sticking point for them was that Rick smoked. It almost could have been the thing that stopped her from even getting to know him. But those eyes, and the way he looked right at her when he talked. And he was so charming! So she ignored the smoking, and at first, he was pretty considerate about where he did it.

But now that he's moved in to her apartment, he is smoking everywhere—in the kitchen, in the living room. Yesterday she walked in and found him smoking in bed! The apartment smells terrible, and her hair and clothes smell like smoke. And he does not seem to care! He just shrugs when she talks about it, pointing out that she was the one who wanted to move in together so soon, making it seem like she is lucky to have him there. He says that it is his home now too, so he should be able to do what he wants.

To make matters worse, he never cleans out any of the ashtrays. They are strewn around the apartment, full, adding to the terrible smell. Last night she found a cigarette butt on the floor! So what did she do? She picked it up. Claudia feels that her personal space has been violated. The more he smokes and the dirtier the apartment gets, she feels like she is losing her own private place in the world, and that is beginning to translate to losing herself. This is similar to Jenna's experience of hiding and eventually losing herself—a common occurrence for Martyrs.

Ask for What You Need

One of the things I hope to achieve in this chapter is to help you come to the point where you dare request the things you need for your own sake and focus on yourself. This will be the challenge. Sometimes, and we will talk about this, it isn't going to be about who is right, but about the simple skill of asserting yourself and putting yourself into the equation. SelfNess is recognizing and appreciating the importance of your own needs and then negotiating for them. It is thinking of yourself—not at the other's expense—but along with the other person. It is overcoming and dismissing the belief that if you take care of your own needs you are being greedy, selfish, uncaring, or unloving.

For example, Claudia needed to be able to set some limits with Rick around where and when he smoked. But before she could do that, she had to feel she had the right to do that. And this is true for so many Martyrs. Sadie stopped going to the gym, someone else might stop going to class, or seeing friends. Laura stopped visiting with her family, because she was always making plans to see Jim's family instead. All of these people need to take self-action and start putting limits in place in order to reclaim time and space for themselves that has been lost to their partners' needs and demands—really, to their partners' selfishness. I don't mean that you have to give up the *we,* but you must find a balance to preserve the *me.* You must put yourself on the page. Jenna did this when she started to go to therapy, which became her space. But it can be many other things too, from making time to take a walk to seeing friends or family to saying no to smoking in your bedroom. This is what you are going to learn how to do.

SelfNess is about learning how to ground yourself in your own needs and not in the needs of others. And this is not easy. I don't mean to say it is. Once you actually take that step, you undoubtedly will feel anxious, because it is a disconnection from the relationship you know. I always tell patients in this situation that it will feel like they have the Emotional Flu. A seasonal flu is caused by a virus, but this one is caused by the separation anxiety you feel once you begin to make these changes. And just as you wash your hands and stay away from sick people, hoping you can escape the fever and congestion of the flu, you have stayed with your partner in an unbalanced situation to avoid this awful Emotional Flu. The fear of separation from the person you love represents a loss: loss of their approval, their love, and what has been your perceived safety and security from which you derive your self-esteem. Every loss brings with it anxiety, the fear of being able to survive without the other person, and the guilt that comes from the concern about whether the other person can survive without you. The symptoms aren't the fever and cough where you feel miserable and can't breathe, but an all-consuming and overwhelming sense of fear, anxiety, guilt, and responsibility.

Both the seasonal flu and the Emotional Flu require that you take time to tend to yourself and take care of yourself, which is another step toward regaining self-importance. This is why you must begin to make changes and put limits in place. When all is said and done, it is a temporary state that will heal. The awful feelings will pass, no matter how bad you feel at the time, just as they did for Jenna. This is a normal part of the process, and it is necessary. Going through this and allowing this to happen is how you develop your emotional muscle. You will use that muscle to manage and tolerate your guilt so you don't have to give in and give up. It is a move toward not accepting the other person's behavior, but rather trying to accept that this is how the other person behaves so that you can determine how you are going to handle yourself. You are building a coping skill. It is part of the process of self-discovery and claiming SelfNess.

Don't Worry, I Understand

Another question you might have to ask yourself is, Are you too forgiving? With so many Martyrs and Givers, they are wronged in one way or another and then they forgive, move on, and let it happen all over again.

Maya let Walker get away with everything: not paying the bills when he said he would, forgetting to call if he was going to be late. She would get mad, of course, and fume when she found the bills unopened on the kitchen table or he promised he would be home for dinner but he wasn't. But every time she had the chance to really give it to him, she backed down. Did she really want to spend the afternoon fighting with him? Or, she would tell herself, dinner was already ruined, was it worth ruining the rest of the night too?

Recently Walker was supposed to pick up Maya at work, and they planned to head out of the city to meet friends for the weekend to hike and enjoy the anticipated nice weather. So Maya left her desk and waited at the side entrance of her building, where Walker always picked her up when he had the car. She waited and waited and kept checking her cell phone. Finally, she decided to go back to her office to make sure he hadn't called her there or maybe even parked and come in to find her. There was no sign of him. When she got back outside again, a good forty minutes after their designated pick-up time, Walker was there. She had brought her suitcase inside when she went back upstairs, but she had left a heavy box of fruit and supplies on the sidewalk. Clearly she was not coming out for the first time, but Walker waved and smiled and she was taken in, as always. What was she going to do? Yell and ruin the drive she was looking forward to? No, it didn't seem worth it. The problem is, while Maya built up resentment, Walker thought he was getting away with something, or at the very least, it didn't occur to him that he was doing anything wrong, because she never told him he was. His inability to follow through and do what he promised was their Selfish Hot Spot (remember those?), but Maya did not have the skills to handle her anger, so she let it go time and time again.

As angry as Maya felt when these things happened, she moved on and forgave but was unable to use the situation to guide her to change what was hurting her in the relationship. And therefore it happened over and over again. When Walker didn't pay the bills, she did it. When he was late or didn't call, she might make a sarcastic comment when he first got home, but she ultimately used forgiveness as her best attempt to cope with it. Rather than acknowledging and attempting to improve this recurring Selfish Hot Spot through dealing with her feelings and setting limits, which I will talk about in more detail soon, she chose instead to be what she considered the bigger person, because it made her feel better about herself.

Maya convinced herself that Walker didn't mean to do these things: it was just because he was easily distracted. She rationalized that it was impossible for him to do everything, and she believed him when he said he needed to get gas or he was stuck at the office or that something had completely slipped his mind. But there is something else going on here. Because Maya is a Martyr and her self-esteem came from doing everything for him, she was getting strength—however unhealthy it might be—each time she let Walker off the hook. Despite her forgiveness, she still felt anger and resentment. She also questioned herself: Was she being unreasonable? Maybe, she decided, so therefore she let it pass without a fight.

Face Your Anger
and Trust Yourself

You must learn to face your anger and hold on to it so it can be a force for change. You must acknowledge your true feelings rather than hide from them, as Maya did. As is typical of a Martyr, Maya has a hard time tapping into her anger. She simply does not feel good about herself when she is angry with her husband—or anybody for that matter. She equates forgiveness with being a good person, and so she forgives constantly.

You must learn to be honest with yourself, and that means accepting your anger, hurt, and disappointment. And that also includes, not only realizing that your partner might be taking advantage of you, but also connecting to your own emotional reality. In other words, if you are so loved by your partner and you are doing what you think you want to be doing, then why are you so unhappy? Once you realize that you still feel miserable despite everything you think you are doing right, you just might be able to find the strength to make some important changes. You can be true to yourself and finally learn to speak your truth. You can then learn to say yes to yourself and no to others through putting boundaries in place.

The real goal for Martyrs and Givers is to be able to give when they are making the choice to genuinely please their partner, not because they are afraid of their partner's anger or their own guilt. Once you have figured out how to manage your guilt so it doesn't hold you back, how to own your anger so you stop making excuses and forgiving your partner no matter what, how to stop giving up all of yourself and your personal time to please your partner, and how to begin to ask for the things you need, you are on the road to SelfNess. You must be personally strong before you can be in a healthy, balanced relationship. You must work on you—that is the *me* in the equation—before you can navigate in the *we*. Your SelfNess comes when your self-worth gives you a sense of self-wealth. And I'm not saying anybody is perfect. So reclaiming yourself means embracing your strengths and your weaknesses. This is how you gain your emotional clarity.

In order to learn to trust yourself, you must become informed. Take the time to answer the following questions by making a list and writing it all down.

What are your strengths and weaknesses? List at least three, but feel free to list more if you want to. Are they valid? Are there more weaknesses than strengths on your list? If so, attempt to balance that.

What are your self-beliefs? The things you beat yourself up about? The common ones I hear are I'm fat, I'm lazy, I'm not smart enough, I'm insecure, I'm always wrong, I'm not good enough. What is on your list? The things you say to yourself over and over to negate your own rights, to tell yourself you don't deserve to be happy. If you are able to identify all these things, then you can not only build your self-esteem through knowing your strengths, but you can identify your trigger points, and you can slowly change your constant need to defend yourself. The goal, then, is to be able to embrace yourself and not berate yourself. By focusing on where you are falling short, you can take steps to develop strength in those areas. You will be stronger, and it won't sting so much when your partner says you are lazy or don't clean enough or don't cook well or have too little patience.

Instead of feeling wounded you can accept your limitations and know you are trying to improve them. Or better yet, you might be able to say, I'm not lazy because I took out the dog and picked up the laundry. You might come to see that it is more about what your partner demands (maybe you did two of the five things on their list) and less about what you actually did. This will help ease the need to constantly prove yourself. If you form your own self-estimation and hold on to your own judgment, your self-esteem will now come from your own approval of yourself and not from the other person's. With that tool you will be able to neutralize your partner's ability to use those attacks as a weapon against you.

This is a crucial step in your progress, because so often, when your partner accuses you of being a certain way in response to a criticism you might have of them or your relationship in general, and you begin to defend yourself, the initial complaint is often lost. Say, for example, that your partner is always late. You finally get the nerve to bring it up, and he turns around and says that you nag him constantly, you never leave him alone! What is wrong with you? There is a skill to dealing with this sort of behavior, and that is to *respond* to his verbal attacks rather than *react* to them. The knee-jerk reaction is to launch into defending yourself against his criticism. But when you do that, you lose the chance to stay focused on what upset you in the first place, in this case that your partner was late. Don't allow yourself to be derailed. Instead, respond to the accusation by saying, as calmly as possible, that you would be willing to talk about the fact that he thinks you nag him at another time, but now you want to talk about his being late.

Examining your childhood will also help you understand who you are so you can finally stop berating yourself. Patients will often tell me about their childhood experiences in such a matter-of-fact way, not at all appreciating the impact that the events had on who they are and how that makes them feel about themselves. My father died when I was fifteen. My parents got divorced when I was six. You really need to pause. It's time for real self-reflection, not just reciting what happened. Take the time and make room to consider what went on when you were a child. And if you start to put value in the fact that your parents got divorced when you were young, or something else made your childhood less than perfect, you might finally be able to, with empathy, realize that you are not feeling sorry for yourself, but you are able to feel the sadness about what you missed out on when you were young. You must be empathetic with yourself before you can be empathetic with a partner.

You will be able to take steps toward securing what you think you missed. Once you connect with your sadness, you can connect with yourself. It is a way to gain security from within yourself instead of depending on your partner to give it to you. It allows you to take ownership and become stronger, more loving and nurturing, and more supportive of yourself, which will transfer to your being in a much healthier relationship.

Allow Yourself to Feel Good

The biggest step in all of this is giving yourself permission to feel good. You must stop associating feeling good with feeling guilty. Doing this will translate to many different things for different people. It means claiming time for yourself. It means taking time out of your day with your family to take a shower or take a walk. It might mean allowing yourself a peaceful cup of coffee each morning or time to read a book in the evening. You have to make time for yourself so that you are not left out. I can't state how vital this is because this will help you reclaim the parts of yourself that have gotten lost along the way. For Sadie it probably means going back to the gym and taking the time again for her daily manicures. Often Martyrs and Givers will think they will give up their needs for a while—while a baby is young, a marriage is new, a business needs help—and then at some point it will be their turn to receive. No! Once the pattern is set, it is very hard to change it. You have to do this now.

I can already hear you saying, "But…but I'm not allowed to," or "But he won't let me." You don't need your partner's permission. You have to get the child out of your head. You are an adult. If you wait for permission, you are never going to get it. So you have to give yourself permission to feel good. You have to reclaim some part of the day as your own. You have to learn how to ask for the things you need. I call this the Speak-Up Skill. The sooner you do each or all of these things, the better.

This is something Lydia is working on. You remember Lydia and Jake. At this moment they are on that slippery slope of losing each other. They haven't had sex in months, and finding their way back to it seems harder and harder at every turn. One thing that might have helped them avoid this dangerous intersection would have been if Lydia had asked for help when she needed it. So often, long before the debacle with the makeup mirror, Lydia would feel that she had to do everything around the house. She paid the bills, she cleaned, she kept the house supplied, she did the laundry. And she was mad and resentful about it. The thing is, Jake had no idea. And she wouldn't say anything until she reached the point of being so angry she couldn't stand it, and then she would lash out.

When Lydia was a child her father was sick. Her mother took care of everyone, the kids and her husband, so that is the role model Lydia grew up with. But her mother also had a lot of pent-up anger. She couldn't yell at her suffering spouse, so often she would suddenly erupt and scream at Lydia. "Why didn't you buy the milk on your way home from school?" "What do you mean you didn't change the sheets?" Lydia would be shocked and stunned every time, because her mother had never asked her to do these things in the first place. Without realizing it, Lydia is treating Jake the way she was treated as a child. This typically happens in a marriage. Jake ends up experiencing the same unpleasant childhood feelings Lydia once had, and he finds it very upsetting, because he doesn't understand where her reactions and behavior are coming from. When Lydia lashes out unexpectedly, as her mother did to her when she was young, it feels random and alien to Jake, and he reacts by feeling angry.

Regularly Lydia would do all the food shopping and then she would carry in the bags. Jake would sometimes be sitting on the front porch, but he wouldn't get up to help. Instead of saying on the first trip in, "Hey, I could use a hand," she grudgingly did it herself. By the third trip she was so furious she would yell.

"Why don't you ever help me?" she would say. "You are always doing what you want to do and not what I need you to do."

Jake would not only be surprised, he would feel stung by her outburst and then quickly become defensive. It never dawned on Lydia that she was acting the way her mother did toward her when she was a child. And she didn't realize that she could simply ask for help. As a Martyr she felt she had to carry all the bags in their marriage, literally. And there was a part of her that wondered, Why should I have to ask? Shouldn't he just know that I need help? The flip side is that Jake honestly didn't realize she needed help, which is not unusual when this tug-of-war plays out in a marriage. Partners of Martyrs often don't realize that their help is wanted. This is typical, lots of people feel this way, and we will talk more about that in the next chapter. But maybe if Lydia had dared to ask, Jake would have readily complied, and one thing wouldn't have led to the other to get them where they are now.

Despite the lines they have drawn, it is not too late for Lydia and Jake. They both want to work at reconnecting. Lydia is taking all the steps we talked about to develop SelfNess (reclaiming herself, working through her guilt, and learning how to better deal with her anger). By doing this she understands that she deserves to be happy, and she has as much right as anyone to ask for the things she wants and needs. She will now be ready for what is to come in chapter 6. Jake has to be ready too. They are both angry with each other on different levels.

In the next chapter you will see the changes she made, the limits she set, how they both learned to talk to each other in a caring manner, and how they were able to make the anger work for them in a constructive way. It is all so simple and yet so hard. Stay with me. Let's see how they and some of the other couples we have met along the way are doing.

Chapter 6

The Language of Love

Heart Talk, Not Hurt Talk

"ARE WE EVER GOING TO HAVE SEX AGAIN?" JAKE ASKED Lydia one night while they were lying coldly next to each other in bed. He hadn't planned on asking. He told himself he was finished even trying with her. But lying there that night, he couldn't help but long for a little warmth from her side of the bed.

"That's up to you," Lydia said flatly.

"Up to me?" Jake asked, sitting up a bit and feeling his tension level begin to rise. "How can it be up to me? Are you saying this is my fault? You're the one who never wants to."

"Me?" Lydia asked, her face getting red. "I wanted to. In fact, the last time sex was even a possibility in this room it was because I initiated it. You turned me down."

"That was after you turned me down a bunch of times," he said angrily. This was exactly why he didn't want to bring it up. She never acknowledged that anything she said or did was upsetting to him. He hated that.

"And that was after you got so mad about that stupid mirror and stopped being nice to me in bed. If anyone shut down around here it was you. So don't start asking *me* if we are ever going to have sex again," she yelled and then got up and left the room. Ugh! He wouldn't give her an inch—ever! She couldn't stand him.

I can't tell you how many times I have heard this conversation or a similar one in my office, either playing out in front of me or repeated back to me by one patient or another.

"You're wrong. I didn't say that."

"No, you're wrong. That is exactly what you said."

"You should get your ears checked. I know what I said and that wasn't it!"

Or, "What are you talking about, I never did that."

"That is exactly what you did!"

I call this the I'm Right, You're Wrong Argument, and it's the heart and soul of the Selfish Game that everyone goes to the mat over. Like Lydia and Jake, each person is feeling blamed by the other, and they are both too busy trying to defend themselves to be able to hear what is being said. And usually the discussion has nothing to do with what is really taking place, because each person locks into the perception of what they think their partner is accusing them of. Very often one or both end up feeling maligned because either they truly believe they didn't actually do what they are being accused of or it was an innocent mistake. But by the way they perceive their partner talking to them, it is as if it was done with criminal intent.

This back and forth of angry disagreement is usually a by-product of misunderstood behavior and intentions. Whether you meant to or not, you may have hurt your partner's feelings in one way or another. So what must happen first and foremost is that you listen to what your partner is actually saying so you can relate to their upset feelings. Once you do that, you can begin to sort through the misconceptions and try to grasp what you may not understand about what the other is saying. Ask your partner to tell you how what you did or what they think you did made them feel. Talk about the impact it had on them, and not about your behavior itself in a judgmental way. For example, say, "When you were late, I felt unimportant and lonely," rather than, "You are rude and think only of yourself (when you were late)." And if you are feeling accused, attacked, or criticized, then you must tell that to your partner and not counter with what you think they did wrong. Next, you want to respond to how they are feeling with, "I'm sorry you're so upset."

I know how difficult this is, and I see my patients grapple with the idea of apologizing when their partner is upset, because they feel it is admitting wrongdoing and they are being unfairly blamed. And most important, they feel that they are being accused of doing something maliciously when often they don't think they did anything wrong in the first place.

Before you can get into the meat of what actually happened between you and your partner, you must first tell your partner that you can understand why they are upset if this is what they really think you did. When you relate to your partner's distress, it is not the equivalent of saying you are wrong, rather it is the first step toward being empathic toward your partner, which is one of the most important tools to have in your belt.

If you don't try to sort out the puzzle of the I'm Right, You're Wrong Argument, all those negative feelings of pain and disappointment remain in play. It will then become next to impossible to dig your way out from under the pile of blame and criticism. Ultimately, the goal is to move from trying to determine *who* is right or wrong to *what* went wrong in your communication, how the misunderstanding between you both occurred. It is up to both of you to figure out where the wires got crossed so you can uncross them and make sure it doesn't happen again.

One of my patients couldn't wait to tell me about the revelation she had just had. During one of the I'm Right, You're Wrong Arguments with her husband, it suddenly dawned on her that he really thought he was right! It made me laugh, because this is something I so often try to convey to my patients. Even though it seems impossible to you that your partner could think they are right about something that is so obviously wrong to you, it is their reality and their truth, and therefore you must deal with it.

The Ace of Hearts Card

Lydia told me about her conversation with Jake and how they spent the next three nights sleeping in separate rooms, furious with each other and barely talking. I decided it was time to share the Ace of Hearts Card. This is a big one, and here is how it works: *A* stands for Acknowledgment, *C* is for Consideration, and the *E* stands for Empathy.

Acknowledge what the problem is according to your partner. This means you must validate what the other person is saying, rather than ignore it or refute it. If, for example, your husband accuses you of interrupting him constantly, then you must acknowledge what he is saying if, in fact, you do interrupt and are aware of it: "You're right. I can see that I do interrupt you at times." Or if you disagree, at least say, "Okay, I understand that you feel interrupted by me, and if that's what you think, I get that you'd be upset. I'm not aware of it, but I'll pay more attention to how much I'm doing it and try to change that." Again, this is not easy, and I tell my patients that the hardest times are when you don't think you are doing something wrong or aren't aware you are doing what you are being accused of. If you don't see it, it is hard to believe it and speak to it. It is easier to play this card when you know you are doing whatever you are being confronted with. The most important thing to remember is that relating empathically to your partner's feelings doesn't automatically make it your fault for how they feel.

Often people don't acknowledge what is going on for this very reason, because they think saying "I'm sorry you feel that way" means "You're right I did do that." But that is not the case. They also hesitate to acknowledge what their partner is saying because they don't want to face the other person's anger. But the truth is, avoiding the problem will only make it worse and also increase your partner's anger and disappointment.

This leads me to the *C* in the Ace of Hearts: Consideration. Consider how what you do and say makes the other person feel. When you tell your partner that you didn't mean to be late—it didn't even occur to you that your husband would be waiting—there is a problem here. You need to consider or be aware of how your behavior affects your partner. So often people will say, "It never occurred to me," and that is part of the problem. It's important to think about how your behavior is going to affect the other person, because the goal is to change the behavior so it doesn't continue in the future. That's the essence of consideration. It's shorthand for saying, "I'm thinking about you, I care about you, and your well-being matters to me." When you don't take the time to consider your partner, that can be at least as hurtful as the actual behavior itself. This is true for all of the Selfish Hot Spot behaviors: forgetting the dishes, staying out late, whatever your Selfish Hot Spot is. The gist is that rather than avoid it, consider and let your partner know you didn't get to what you said you were going to do, or you did something they don't like, so they can deal with it accordingly. Finally, the person who wants the consideration must agree to not jump down their partner's throat when they get it. If your partner never calls to say he will be late but tells you that he will, when he does call, you want to say, "I'm glad you called." You can be upset with him for being late, but you can't lash out in anger and attack him. At least he was able to show you some consideration so you are no longer in the dark, and now you can take some control of the situation by putting a limit in place. For example, you can choose to eat dinner without him, instead of waiting while the dinner gets cold, expecting him to walk in at any minute. This idea of setting limits is something I will talk more about as we move through the chapter.

And finally the *E* in the Ace of Hearts: Empathize with your partner. I call this "giving the tin man a heart." Empathy is when you use your heart and compassion so the emotional oil of love can flow between you and help you understand what the other person is going through. It enables you to think about how your partner feels and how what you do affects them. It would be like putting yourself in your partner's shoes. This helps you become emotionally connected to them in a heartfelt way. It pulls you out of your all-consuming anger. Empathy lays the groundwork for being able to jointly problem solve, which we will talk about in chapter 8.

Until now you may think you were talking to each other, but you were really talking at each other: attacking, blaming, and finding fault. Consequently, it's difficult to really listen to what is coming out of your partner's mouth without jumping in to talk over him. I call this Assault with a Verbal Weapon. This is the way Lydia and Jake talked to each other for too long, the way they talked to each other in bed that night when each thought he or she was right but the other was wrong, with no room to consider the other person at all. When this happens, each partner hears only what they think their partner is saying rather than what is actually being said. The misunderstood conversation leads to disappointment. The attempt itself to talk about whatever the problem is leads to angry reactions that create distance, just as it did in bed that night for Lydia and Jake and the nights of sleeping apart that followed. The goal is to be able to genuinely listen to each other, which means making sure you stick to talking about your own feelings and not your partner's faults.

If Lydia and Jake can really learn to play the Ace of Hearts—and if you can in your own relationship—so much of the anger and resentment and negativity will slip away, and you and your partner will have many more consistently positive interactions. I tell my patients to put down the BAT—the Blame, Attack, and Trigger—you use to provoke each other. The reason so many people resort to using the BAT is because they don't have the skills they need to deal with their anger. When you club each other with the BAT, as Lydia and Jake did at the beginning of this chapter, no one ever feels understood. As I mentioned earlier, instead of throwing criticism back at your partner—clubbing back—ask them to tell you how they are feeling instead of what they think of you.

When Jake asked angrily if they were ever going to have sex again, Lydia would have been better off saying something like, "Look, you're really mad and upset, and I can see that, but I'm feeling attacked and criticized. Can you tell me what you are so upset about?" When you ask your partner to tell you the impact your behavior had on him, how it made him feel, the discussion becomes, "I'm angry because you haven't wanted to have sex in a month, and I feel unloved," instead of, "You are cold and selfish (or inconsiderate or thoughtless)." Without that honesty, there is nothing to gain but distance and disconnection.

That day in my office, Lydia listened and nodded and said she would try. The following week she came in smiling and told me about the conversation she and Jake had the night after our last session.

Her first big step was that she was willing to break the ice with Jake and initiate a conversation, instead of remaining locked in a standoff, which was her old style.

"I know you are upset with me because we haven't had sex in a while," she said. (*Acknowledge.*) "I know I have been so focused on work and all the stuff I have to get done, and I've felt exhausted and overloaded, so that's why I've been shutting you down when you reached out to me. (*Consider.*) I know you are feeling rejected by me, but that is not how I want you to feel. I want to be with you sexually, and I want us to be happy together." (*Empathy.*)

Jake was floored. He was scared after the nights of sleeping in separate rooms. He knew that was not leading anywhere good. As angry as he was, he didn't think he wanted to leave Lydia. He was eager to find a way to share their lives together peacefully and happily. But he couldn't begin to figure out how they would get through the mess. So when she talked to him that way, he felt a huge wave of relief. And he was able to take a deep breath and play his own Ace of Hearts Card. He told her that he knew he was retaliating when he turned on her and rejected her attempt at sex (*Acknowledgment*). He didn't realize that his not helping around the house was so burdensome to her, since he saw her as capable and full of energy (*Consideration*). He wanted her to feel supported and appreciated and not resentful, and he told her he would be willing to help out (*Empathy*).

This goes right back to a few of the points I made in chapter 5, that you have to ask for help when you need it, and you have to do so before you get so angry you explode. You have to understand that your partner does not always know and anticipate this need for help—he simply can't. Many people have the expectation that, "He *should know*, so why do I have to ask?" "She *should know*, so why do I have to ask?" The notion that our partners will know what we want without our having to put it into words is a carryover from infancy when we had no choice but to depend on our parents to "know" when we were hungry or cold or tired, because we weren't able yet to talk. As an adult, though, you now have the ability and power to convey your needs verbally. It is important that you tell your partner what you want from them. This way you take care of yourself proactively instead of passively waiting for them to guess what you need, which only perpetuates your remaining dependent, feeling helpless, and becoming angrier.

A lot of times people think telling their partner what they wish for or asking their partner for what they need is about taking care of their partner, making it easier for them. Or that somehow if you tell your partner what you want, and then they follow through, it has less meaning and the behavior is less authentic, because you had to ask for it. In truth, though, it is about your taking self-responsibility, and if your partner listens to you and is able to give you what you ask for, that is great. And there are times you might want to encourage your partner so that he can use the Help Me Help You Pitch, as we saw in the movie *Jerry Maguire*, if you anticipate that he might flounder and need direction. In other words, if you are going to be out at night and want your husband to feed the kids and put them to bed, why not either leave dinner for him to reheat or suggest he order pizza? It will allow your partner to not be so overwhelmed, and it will better help him to help you. You can leave the kids' pajamas on their beds while you're at it.

Along the same lines, sometimes when you do ask your partner to load the dishwasher, fold the laundry, or feed the kids, his immediate response may be to accuse you of not liking the way he does it or even of redoing it when he has done it in the past. When this comes up in my office, I tell my patients that that is not unusual, so what you want to do is tell your partner how you like it to be done, or if he isn't sure, encourage him to ask you if you have a preference. The third choice here is to simply accept his difference in style. There has to be a give-and-take, and the asking and accepting has to go both ways.

Think of it this way, miscommunication is like a bad back scratch. Your left shoulder itches, you can barely stand it, so you ask your partner to scratch your back. She is happy to, but she goes for the middle of your back. It feels good, but that itch on your shoulder is getting worse. You think she is going to move in that direction at any time and you wait. What is taking her so long? Despite her good intentions, you are getting annoyed. You think she knows what you want, but she doesn't. You must be clear and direct. Tell your partner where it itches! Tell her from the get-go. Then there won't be any confusion or frustration, and your miscommunication will be gone. Your expectations need to be stated clearly, then she can genuinely please you. And of course, you aren't in this alone, so sometimes your partner can ask you where it itches to make sure she is hitting the right spot—again, the give-and-take.

The Rules of Engagement: Fair Play

These are other important skills that will help you and your partner communicate smoothly. I call them the Rules of Engagement, and they include a few very useful tools.

Rule Number 1: Make a Request

Make a Request of your partner rather than a demand. This is so important. One of my patients, Tess, recently realized this about the asking that goes on in her family. You remember Tess and Pablo, right? They are still struggling over the question of which religion to raise their girls and all the issues that that has brought up. Tess wants to talk about it all the time, but Pablo shuts down. They are making some progress, but on this particular day Tess told me a story about her daughter Celia. She and Pablo are always after the girls to brush their teeth. It was a constant battle. Sometimes, they would have to ask them more than ten times to brush their teeth, and you can imagine what that ninth and tenth demand sounded like.

The other day, during one of these battles, Celia turned to Tess and said, "Can we have a conversation about this, Mommy?" It was something that I have encouraged Tess and Pablo to say to each other in their attempt to work through things. They are starting to understand that it is okay to disagree, but not without an honest conversation.

Tess was taken aback by Celia's not only picking up on that tactic but the maturity of asking to use it.

"Sure," Tess said to her seven-year-old daughter. "Let's talk."

"Why is it that you and Daddy are always making demands? Everything is a demand. Would it kill either of you to say 'please'?"

What could Tess say? When she thought about it for a minute, it made total sense to her. She promised Celia that she would do her best to say please and to ask her and her sister to do something whenever that was possible, instead of telling them to do it. She promised also to pay attention to the tone of her voice.

When Tess relayed the conversation to me, my first thought was, "From the mouths of babes." This is a basic skill I teach to my patients, the first in the Rules of Engagement. I can't say this enough: I want my patients to learn how to Make a Request rather than a demand. Simply put, ask nicely. This conveys basic respect for your partner and offers your partner the ability to make a choice. When you make a demand of your partner, they often feel manipulated, coerced, and controlled by you, because there is the sense that they must do what you are telling them to do. When you Make a Request, however, it frees your partner and allows them to make a choice, acting, hopefully, on their genuine desire to please you. Even as a child, as you can see with Celia, when it is, in fact, the parents' job to tell you what to do, there is still hope for respect that will then allow that child to cooperate on her own. Which is to say, she feels she is making her own choice. This way, you avoid setting up a power struggle that becomes a *me* versus *you* Selfish Showdown.

When Lydia came to see me the following week, I shared all of this with her. I told her that if she is constantly waiting until she is already angry with Jake and then making demands of him, not only is he immediately put on the defensive, but he is not being given a choice in the matter. They must learn to give each other the power of choice. If something is presented in a nice way and as a request, the other person can then take ownership and responsibility and feel that they *want to do* whatever it is for their partner, not that they *have to do*. In an adult relationship, this allows you to move away from a parent-child dynamic and into an equal partnership. It is a complement to the Ace of Hearts Card.

Rule Number 2: Play Emotional Jeopardy

Before you make a statement based on your assumptions that often sounds like you are accusing your partner of something, first ask what is going on with them. It is what I call *Play Emotional Jeopardy*. Put your concern in the form of a question and check it out, and your partner won't feel attacked and then become defensive and attack you back. Doing this allows you to set up an open conversation in which you can truly find out what did or didn't happen. This helps develop the trust that you are not out to get each other or exhibiting the negative behavior intentionally. When you don't check things out is when you will have real jeopardy on your hands.

For example, instead of Laura's accusing Jim of thinking only of himself when he came home recently with tickets to a show that was not the one they discussed seeing, she decided to Play Emotional Jeopardy and ask him about it. It turns out that he tried very hard to get tickets to the show she wanted to see, even considering missing a night meeting so they could go, but the show was almost completely sold out, and there were only single tickets left throughout the theater. He wanted to sit with her! So he chose another musical, a production she had mentioned being interested in. In the past, she might have jumped all over him and accused him of not thinking of her at all, but in fact, he was trying very hard to be thoughtful. Playing Emotional Jeopardy helps to untangle what is going on between two people and allow for understanding. Stop assuming you know why your partner acts a certain way. Let go of the idea that he did it on purpose or was trying to get back at you for something. Ask first!

Very often what might be at play in these situations of misunderstanding is the Wild Card Factor (when something unexpected happens that throws everything out of whack): someone gets sick, there were no pairs of tickets available, a tire went flat on the drive home. In spite of the most thought-out plans and best intentions, you have to be prepared for something to come up, and you have to be able to talk about it if it does, rather than remaining mad about what's gone wrong. Try to pinpoint the Wild Card and separate it from the rest of what is going on. For example, if your partner always bows out of plans at the last minute, and you are always annoyed by that, and then one day he gets sick and has to bow out, you have to acknowledge that this is different from your normal Selfish Hot Spot issue. When Jim went to get the tickets for Laura, and there were no two seats together, he encountered the Wild Card, even though he had the best of intentions. Try to make sure you know what the situation was and talk about what happened, as Jim and Laura were able to do, rather than let it confuse an already confusing situation. Playing Emotional Jeopardy is the skill that will help you put down your Judgment Mirrors.

Rule Number 3: Hit the Hold Button

You can't always talk about everything the minute you want to, so it helps to know that you can *Hit the Hold Button*. It is important to determine when to talk in the moment to easily resolve something and when to decide to talk at another time. The skill here is to know when to put things on hold. Sometimes this is more challenging, especially when your partner gives you the Now or Never Threat, meaning if you don't talk to me now, I won't talk to you later. Even though your partner might make you anxious that they won't have a conversation with you at another time, it is important to recognize that you can claim some control for yourself by trusting that you can shut down the conversation at that point and revisit it later. Try to be empathic. Let your partner know you understand where they are coming from, and also express your own situation at the moment, that you are too tired or overloaded, and finally set up a time in the future that you can both look forward to when you can finish your discussion.

Hitting the Hold Button is a handy little tool that can be used at any point when one person is angry and the other is unwilling or unable to talk or if it is not an appropriate time to have the discussion (you have just arrived at a party, are out to dinner with friends, or it is too late at night to get into it). Agree together, so you are part of the same team. If you arrive at that party and you are in the middle of an argument, don't jump out the minute the car stops and slam the door. Instead, take a deep breath, acknowledge with your partner that you are both upset, and decide on a time you can continue the discussion in a mindful, planned way instead of erupting at inopportune times when there is no chance to resolve your issue. Think of it as a bridge over your troubled water. Not only does it carry you from the Selfish Hot Spot moment to your next discussion, it also builds in some cooldown time and might let you both enjoy the party. It can be used to tame and manage the Never-Ending Fight because it gives you the structure to talk about it thoughtfully instead of engaging in a selfish circular argument. Hopefully, when you get back to the issue at hand, you will be in a calmer place so you can talk in a more caring way.

This takes me back to Tess and Pablo, who often encountered a problem when Tess felt the immediate need to talk, but Pablo didn't want to because he was too upset. Now they know how to Hit the Hold Button, and therefore "having a conversation" is often simply talking about when they are going to talk. If

Tess says she wants to talk now, and Pablo says he doesn't, then they can acknowledge each other's needs and decide together on a time that would work for both of them. He can offer her a specific time. If he doesn't want to talk that afternoon, maybe he will suggest they talk after work on Friday, when they have had a day to think about it and the work week is over. That way, rather than resulting in an argument, Pablo no longer feels backed into a corner, and Tess no longer feels rejected. Because he acknowledges that she wants to talk instead of avoiding it altogether, she is able to relax and let go instead of continuing to bombard him with the conversation. And now Tess can look forward to the time they set to talk. They are working together as a team.

Can it be that simple? Talking nicely to your partner, saying please, asking instead of demanding, checking out where your partner is coming from instead of assuming, knowing when to put your conversation on hold, acknowledging them, considering them, and empathizing with them? Yes and no. Most people don't enter the conversation until they are already fed up with the other person, which is often when people become self-righteous. Each person attempts to outdo the other with who is the most upset and who has the most "right" to be angry, because they feel so wronged. A lot of times, Martyrs and Givers, because they feel guilty about their needs or don't want to make trouble, let their annoyance build until it reaches a point where they feel they have a right to be mad, and then they use their anger to justify attacking their partner. It then becomes a matter of who can say the most hurtful things. Martyrs and Givers can be more suscep-tible to becoming self-righteous, because they tend to sit on their anger and tolerate a lot, letting their guilt rule the roost. You do have the right to be mad; in fact, it is important that you are in touch with it. But it is equally important that you express your anger in a constructive way so that you can use it to make your relationship better.

Communication and Expectation

When couples come into my office with a problem, and I say, "We need to talk about this," they usually respond, "We've been talking about this for years. It doesn't help, it doesn't make a difference." They think they are talking, but the truth is that they are not getting through to each other, because the Assault with a Verbal Weapon is taking its toll, and they end up stuck and frustrated.

Much of the problem has to do with a difference in expecta-tions, similar to the ones we talked about in chapter 2. As we know, Martyrs, Givers, Takers, and Controllers all manifest their needs in different ways. In the same way that people don't know which of their expectations are realistic and which ones warrant the need for compromise—and sometimes Takers and Controllers never give any thought to it, believing every one of their expectations is valid and should be fulfilled—people's expectations of how to talk to each other and share their feelings often clash. And the expectations of how the other person should listen and respond often explode in their faces.

Mixing different expectations with miscommunication is a recipe for disaster. Couples typically end up trying to get their respective cases heard without really listening to their partner. They end up blaming themselves and feeling guilty (I'm asking for too much; I'm being too selfish) or blaming their partner (Why is this all about him and his needs? Why doesn't he ever listen to me?). Either way, this can cause an emotional disconnect.

And then there are the communication styles themselves. One person gets their feelings out by being biting and sarcastic (Augustine) while his partner (Rose) becomes withdrawn and sullen. Or one partner (Tess) makes demands while the other (Pablo) avoids the topic at all costs. The truth is, couples can talk around or talk at an issue for years without ever talking through it.

Let's look quickly at how Martyrs, Givers, Takers, and Controllers can differ in their expectations and communication styles.

Martyr

Expectations: The Martyr doesn't ever expect that their partner will come through for them. In fact, if their partner does try to give to them, verbally or in any other way, they will often feel uncomfortable and try to push their partner away. They feel a tremendous sense of responsibility for their partner's needs, but they also feel most powerful and in control when they are giving and taking care of another person.

Communication style: Martyrs are afraid to ask for anything, so they don't. If they do, it's typically in the form of being out of control—either in a big fight or after a few glasses of wine. While they don't make any verbal demands or even requests, they are often quite good manipulators. Their silence can be the only tool they use to get what they want.

On the rare occasions that Monica spoke up to Leonard, specifically about where she wanted to live after they had a baby, he shut her down and blamed her. I am not going to go into the details here because I do so in the next chapter, and for them it does not end well. But that doesn't have to be the case. Some Martyrs are able to take the control that is necessary and set those limits we keep talking about.

Giver

Expectations: Givers mostly look to give to their partner and meet their needs, but they do expect something in return. They're inclined to give in to the desire to keep score of what they've given and get in return, tit for tat, so to speak.

Communication style: Givers will verbally request things of their partner, but if their needs aren't met, they will get very hurt and disappointed and feel as if it's not fair. They often think, *After all I've done for you, how can you not do this one thing for me?*

Laura has felt for a long time that she has given up so much for Jim in an effort to show him that she would be a great wife. But Jim takes advantage of her and doesn't feel like he ever really has to follow through with the plans they make, because he is certain she will tolerate pretty much anything he does.

"I am really upset," she finally told him. "I know you think you'll do the things you say you will, but you never do. I give you so much without your ever having to ask. Why do I always have to ask you?"

Taker

Expectations: Takers expect that when they ask their partner to do something, their partner will say yes. They are often unaware of what they are asking, oblivious of the extra time or effort it would entail for their partner, which can make them appear rude or inconsiderate.

Communication style: Takers have no trouble verbalizing their requests, but they often do it with blame or criticism instead of in a loving, caring way.

Jerome is a Taker. As we've seen repeatedly with Tina and Jerome, he is not afraid to ask for a thing. He decorates the house the way he wants to and always wants her to initiate sex. Things are pretty one-sided for them, and so is the way they have been talking to each other.

"I thought you liked baseball," he said accusingly when she questioned if they really needed a fifth print of the Yankees in their den. "You've never complained before. What's the problem now?"

Controller

Expectations: Controllers expect that they are going to get exactly what they want once they make it known to their partner. And should their partner have any needs of their own that they may try to introduce into the conversation, it will result in the Controllers' anger and questioning your love for them.

Communication style: Controllers don't request, they inform. "We're leaving at seven." "We're going to Orlando for vacation." If their partner resists or protests, they are quick to get angry. In order to control their partner they will sulk in silence or become furious. They also commonly devalue their significant other by saying, "It's no big deal," or "You're making something out of nothing," and the partner then questions their own feelings.

When Claudia tells Rick that she is unhappy with his smoking all over the house, he barely listens and moves the conversation around to how lucky she is to have him there and, frankly, how much he has given up to be there.

"I really hate the smell of smoke, and I am starting to hate even coming home," she told him recently.

"Why are you making an issue about it now. It was no secret that I smoke," he answered. "My cigarettes are part of the package. You can't expect me to stop smoking now. If you loved me, you would never ask me to do that."

Ultimately by being clear about the expectations and the different communication styles of the Martyrs, Givers, Takers, and Controllers, you can change the way you talk to each other so that the communication between you will flow more freely.

The Ace of Hearts in Play

I can go down the line of many of the patients I have told you about and show you how playing the Ace of Hearts Card has helped, no matter which group they fall into. Nina was able to acknowledge that she interrupted Geoff, which opened the door for everything else to flow. Lacey acknowledged that she called Chase names and came to understand how much that bothered him. Augustine finally came to see he had an anger issue, and once he recognized that, he was able to take the necessary steps to soften his reactions. By owning their behavior it validates the impact it is having on their partner, which can eventually help stop the fighting. Each, in their Acknowledgment, takes responsibility for their upsetting behavior rather than denying, negating, countering, or retaliating. By doing so, their partner will feel related to, because they are making their behavior real.

Takers and Controllers need to acknowledge their selfish and entitled behavior, and Givers and Martyrs must flex the emotional muscle they have developed and put limits in place. As we discussed in chapter 5, Claudia has to start setting limits. People hear these words—setting limits or putting boundaries in place—and they are confused by what that means. The common assumption is that putting limits in place means telling the other person to stop the behavior that is bothering you. Not true. Setting limits means using your anger to first realize something is wrong, and then *you* take the necessary steps and make the necessary changes. You must push back in a constructive way and be clear about what you will and will not accept. Stop trying to control your partner's behavior, and instead use your anger to take action and control for yourself.

Claudia realized how furious she was—she had lost her space, her home stunk—and it didn't seem fair. Add in the fact that the smoke was really starting to bother her physically—her allergies were flaring up and she woke up each morning feeling short of breath—and she was as angry as ever. When things begin to seem unfair between you and your partner, when you feel taken for granted or mistreated, that is a good indication that you need to set limits or define boundaries. Just do something! This is exactly what happened with Claudia, and this is how she began to make things better.

"I understand smoking is important to you," she finally told Rick, "but we both live here, and if we are going to continue to live together, can you either go outside to smoke like you do at work, or how about you can smoke inside if I'm not here? But if you do smoke when I'm at home, I'm going to have to leave the room in order to protect my health. If we're talking or hanging out or watching a movie, I will not be able to continue to do that while you smoke. It is just too upsetting and too hazardous for me."

Similarly, Laura had that same feeling that things were unfair in her relationship with Jim. As you know, she did mostly everything in their relationship, and Jim almost never stuck to the plans they made. So she, too, began to set limits. She was very mindful to not tell him what to do but rather what she was going to do if he continued with what she saw as negative behavior. He rarely washed the dishes, for example, even when he said he was going to. Laura found this stressful because she spent the night tense, wondering when and if he was going to get to it. So she finally told him she would rather he just say he wasn't going to and instead they could switch to using paper plates occasionally. That would be good for both of them, she added. And she also told him that when they agreed on a plan—that they would go home right after a movie or that they would hang out with her friends on a given night—he should ask her before making any changes so that she was clearly considered. Then she could decide if she wanted to go along with the changes or if she would follow through with the original plans without him. If he didn't ask her, she added, she would go along with the initial plans they had set. That way, she could know what to expect and she wouldn't get so mad.

Once Jim acknowledged how upset Laura was about his constantly changing or not following through with the plans, she felt heard and understood. Instead of blaming him, she Played Emotional Jeopardy and asked him openly if he was doing it on purpose because he didn't care. And he was able to answer without being defensive, because he didn't feel attacked.

"I never change the plans intentionally for the sake of changing the plans," he said. "For some reason something always seems to come up, or something I don't expect happens." He was able to tell her in such a way that she could understand that the Wild Card was in play for him.

"Well, when that happens, at least let me know so I can plan accordingly," she said. That was their Acknowledgment. Next came Consideration: Jim promised to think about Laura before he made any decisions affecting their plans, and she agreed to try to think about how the plans they made might affect him.

Finally, Empathy: Jim was able to tell Laura that he understood how hard this had been for her. "I feel bad that you've been upset. That's not how I want you to feel. Here is what I'll do about it. I'll try my best to follow through with the plans we make and when I can't, I'll talk to you about it and explain what is going on with me."

Love You, Mean It
Hate You, Mean It
Moments

Using these skills will help you stay connected to your loving feelings. However, many couples I see find that even when things are good between them, it is sometimes impossible to always and only have these loving feelings. They find that their feelings often flip into negative ones where they may, at times, even feel like they "hate" their partner. This is known as Ambivalence and is, in fact, a common element that exists in every relationship. Most people are unaware of it, because when they get married, they expect their partner to love them all the time, unconditionally, no matter what they say or do. In return, they will love them the same way. But that doesn't happen. The reality of an adult love relationship is that loving feelings often are conditional and based on how your partner treats you and how you treat your partner. Positive behavior generates the Love You, Mean It moments, and negative behavior brings with it the Hate You, Mean It moments. It is easy for the bad to pile up and eclipse the good and for the Hate You, Mean It moments to take over. And you can have both feelings in one day, even in the same hour! When all is said and done, selfish behavior can make you, at times, feel like you hate your partner. Those Hate You, Mean It moments, which of course are born out of anger, can make you feel guilty and see yourself as a bad person for feeling them, but the truth is, it is natural to experience them. There is always an ebb and flow in every relationship. If you know this ambivalence is going to be there, it won't be a surprise or so confusing. Accept it and use it as a tool to help manage your anger. In other words, instead of lashing out with blame and everything else, you can simply say, "Hate You, Mean It," to let off some steam. When you both agree, you can use it as shorthand or as Morse code to clue the other person into how upset you are while lightening the mood. It can be used in jest to lessen the intensity of any situation. Know also that these Hate You, Mean It moments can be balanced with Love You, Mean It moments, especially when you bring the Ace of Hearts into play so that you turn the minus in your hand into a plus with Acknowledgment, Consideration, and Empathy.

Remember Fran and Clark who were caught up in the "I'll See Your Stress and Raise You" Selfish Hot Spot? Both of them were so desperate to be understood that they were unwittingly negating each other's feelings. Whenever Clark would counter Fran with his own stressful day, she would feel a Hate You, Mean It moment and want to avoid him, and he felt the same way about her. For Fran and Clark, empathy was what was missing. They began to use the Hate You, Mean It statement as their Morse code to let the other know they were angry and needed some understanding. And when she said, "Hate You, Mean It," to Clark it took the fire out of her distress. Once they saw what they were doing to each other, all it took for them was to slow down and say, "Wow, you had a hard day! I can see why you are feeling so stressed. You did so much!" So simple, yet so powerful. This ushered in the Love You, Mean It moments and helped them feel connected to each other.

Changing Your Hand

No matter how hot your Selfish Hot Spots are and no matter how long your Never-Ending Fight has been going on, if you and your partner are committed to making it work, you can change the relationship for the better using the tools and skills I gave you in this chapter: Play the Ace of Hearts, remember the Rules of Engagement so that you can Make a Request rather than a demand, Hit the Hold Button, Play Emotional Jeopardy, look for the Wild Card in play, and set the limits you need. You will be able to truly listen to each other, talk to each other, and really understand one another, and most important, feel understood and supported by each other so that you will have the desire and cooperative spirit to problem solve and move toward a workable compromise. If you, in fact, feel supported and understood, you will find that you will truly want to please your partner. You will learn to speak the language of love so your partner remains your lover and your ally, and you will transform your hurt talk into Heart Talk. These tools will give you the hose you need to put out all of those nasty Selfish Hot Spots.

Here is what happened in Lydia and Jake's kitchen recently. She planned to make an easy chicken and dumpling recipe for dinner, but of course, it was more complicated than she thought. It involved rolling out dough. A month ago—even two weeks ago—she would have suffered through, probably reaching her boiling point just as dinner was about to be served. But not that night. Jake was watching the news in the next room.

"Would you mind helping me with this dough?" she called. She heard the TV click off, and then he was at her side.

"Sure, what do I have to do?"

Together they made the dough, and Jake rolled it out while she simmered the chicken. He stayed with her for the rest of the dinner preparation, setting the table without her having to ask him to. And the hour was actually fun, not a chore at all.

The next night, before she had to even wonder where he was or what he was doing, he came into the kitchen. He was there to help form the burgers and turn on the grill. They listened to music and touched each other gently as they moved by each other with ketchup and mustard and tongs to turn the burgers, which were delicious. He washed the dishes while she swept the floor. And guess what they did that night? You guessed it: they had sex.

Chapter 7

What's the Bottom Line?

MONICA LAY DOWN FOR THE FIRST TIME IN OVER TWENTY hours. Had it really been that long? The apartment was quiet, and she went through the long hours in her mind. It was almost 8:00 p.m. now, and it had been about midnight last night when the baby woke up screaming. After the entire night and much of the day of trying everything she could think of—rocking, singing, nursing, riding up and down in the elevator—she made a late afternoon trip to the pediatrician to find out the baby was teething. A little Tylenol, a frozen teething ring, and sleep was finally achieved.

Monica settled under the covers just as she heard the front door open. Leonard was home. He had slept through much of last night and showed some concern this morning, but she hadn't heard from him all day. She left him a voice mail letting him know the official diagnosis, just in case he had been as worried as she that there was something really wrong. But he hadn't called back. She considered quickly turning out the light so it would be clear she was done for the night, but she worried he would catch her. So she waited with her eyes closed.

It didn't take long. Within minutes he was in the doorway of the bedroom and staring at her. She knew she wouldn't be able to pretend to be asleep for long if he kept standing there. He cleared his throat. Then he noisily took off his tie and his jacket and sighed heavily. He removed his shoes and threw them, not really hard but hard enough to make a thud, toward his closed closet door.

Her eyes shot open.

"You're going to wake the baby," she said, more anger in her voice then she had meant there to be.

"Is that the welcome I get?" he asked, plenty of anger in his voice. "I come home from a long day of working so you can have the luxury to stay home and care for our child, and that's how you say hello? How about, 'Hi honey, I missed you. You must be exhausted.'"

Monica took a deep breath. This was the last thing she wanted to do now. She closed her eyes and tried to settle back down. Maybe he would walk away. He didn't.

"So what's for dinner?"

She sighed and sat up.

"I don't know if you got my message, but the baby is teething. Apparently teething can be enough to warrant twenty hours of screaming. This is the first time I've put him down. I haven't eaten all day. I haven't thought about dinner."

"Well, just cause he's teething doesn't mean I'm going to starve," Leonard said.

"Can't you see I need to sleep?" she lashed out.

"Well I need to eat!"

"Could you, maybe, make some pasta? Or a tuna sandwich? Or what about bringing something in? I'm pretty hungry too, I guess," she said, less angrily.

"Oh, so now I'm supposed to work all day *and* make dinner? I don't think so. What happened to my wife? You're supposed to think of me too. What is going on with you?"

Guilt flashed through her for a moment. What was wrong with her? But she quickly pushed it to the side; she could finally see that there was nothing wrong with her. There was something wrong with him. She wished she had tried harder to feign sleep, because she was way too tired to think about this now. She had reached the end of the line with Leonard and she knew it. She had known it for a while, actually. The last few times she didn't do things exactly his way and then tried to rationally explain her reasons for that, and he had followed with his usual Bottom Line of threatening to leave, she actually found herself wondering if that would really be so bad. For most of their relationship, his threats had instilled pure fear in her. She didn't want to live without him. But since the baby had been born, well, she was really starting to wonder. Monica had had lots of very good reasons for not doing things perfectly around the house lately, and yet he was completely unable to empathize with her. She finally realized that no matter what, Leonard truly thought only of himself, even when she was sick when the baby was about a month old. He took him for an hour while he was quiet and happy, and then he forced Monica out of bed to help when he became fussy. If he ever gave her an inch—she had started to take notice of this during the last six months—it was only when it served him or met his own needs. And to make things worse, he acted like he had given her the world! He still talked about how he took care of the baby when she was sick.

"You never ever think of me," Monica heard herself say. "I have been up for two days, and before that, I was going on very little sleep! How can you not see that I am overwhelmed and exhausted? I'm not a robot. I can't do everything I am doing now and everything I did before the baby came. It is not humanly possible!"

He was quiet for a minute. Could she have finally gotten through to him? *Oh, please*, she thought to herself.

"So what's for dinner?" he finally asked. Eerily he spoke in the same tone he had when he first asked, as though this conversation had never taken place, as though she hadn't just pleaded with him to understand where she was coming from.

"I want a divorce," Monica said. She realized later that it was almost seven years exactly after she had said "I do" so hopefully.

He laughed a bit, not believing her words. He was so sure she would never leave him. Surely she was just using his Bottom Line tactic. But she got up, grabbed her pillow, and spent the night on the floor of the baby's room. The next morning she packed a few things and took the baby to stay with her mother. She knew she was moving toward the end. Despite years of trying to improve her marriage, she finally realized she could not do it alone.

There are times, sadly, when there is literally no way to get through to your partner, when you could follow every one of these rules, but your partner won't budge. And even though you are holding on to hope or the fear of change keeps you in the relationship, those are the times when the best thing to do for you might be to get out. You think there is something wrong with you, that it is your own personal failure, but that isn't the case when you have tried your best to implement the tools and skills we talked about in this book. You find yourself up against a brick wall because your partner is completely uncooperative. This is when you are dealing with what I call an Ultimate Controller. This person cannot and will not hear you. That is the bottom line.

In these situations, the partner who won't give an inch constantly threatens to leave the relationship when there is any attempt to confront them or change behavior. There is absolutely no room for a give-and-take. Leonard did this over and over again during their marriage, threatening to walk out when the slightest thing made him angry. Playing the "I'm Leaving" Deal Breaker Card was his way of maintaining power and control. And it worked for a long time. Leonard never got it. He never understood what Monica needed or where she was coming from, and he refused to own up to his behavior.

Leonard is an Ultimate Controller, and he isn't the only one. This is a Controller who takes their behavior to the extreme, and regardless of whether they're dealing with emotional or sexual needs, it's always all about them. They are so consumed by their own needs that nobody else exists. As we saw with Monica and Leonard, they view their partners as objects there to exclusively satisfy their needs. Their dominant emotion is anger, and they use it to maintain a tight reign to keep the other person in the relationship. In fact, almost all of their actions stem from anger. Their sense of entitlement is profound. They think they have the right to anything and everything they want from you. When their needs aren't met, they are quick to explode. It is their way of completely shutting down and refusing to deal with compromise in any way, shape, or form.

However long you wait for approval and understanding from an Ultimate Controller—as Monica did for so long—is how long you will be unhappy. As I talked about in my book *Gridlock: Finding the Courage to Move on in Love, Work and Life,* the more you try to reason with your unreasonable partner, the more you will stay stuck, because your hope for them to hear you is unrealistic. As long as you hold on to that hope, you become as unreasonable in your demand of them as they are of you with their demands. They cannot hear you or understand your needs, and they have no wish to, so your attempts to get through to them go absolutely nowhere. No matter how hard you try to fix it, you just can't. It's like screaming in an empty forest. Your partner will never hear you, no matter how loud you shout. An Ultimate Controller will deny your reality; the only reality that exists for them is their own. You have to be able to take your understanding of what you know to be true, whether your partner can see it or not, and act on it, as Monica has finally done. To remain in a marriage or relationship with an Ultimate Controller often means completely sacrificing yourself.

As we saw with Monica, people who are with Ultimate

Controllers often feel they are walking on eggshells and will do anything to avoid their partner's outbursts, which often lead to the Bottom Line threat of leaving. They constantly feel as if they have to prove themselves, like they can lose their partner's love at the drop of a hat, which is exactly how their partner wants them to feel. There is a constant bombardment of attacks from their partner. Leonard was angry every time things didn't go his way. Monica was motivated for so long by Leonard's constant threat of abandonment—losing his love and what she saw as the security of their relationship weighed over her.

No matter how hard someone might work to make a marriage or relationship healthy and equal, Ultimate Controllers only give back just enough to keep you satisfied so that you will continue to keep giving to them. We saw this with Leonard's taking the baby for the briefest periods of time. But when he gave the baby back, he was clearly angry with Monica for needing even that bit of time to herself. Ultimate Controllers become angry with their partners for having needs of their own. Similarly, when Monica was too tired to deal with dinner, in Leonard's eyes, her exhaustion simply didn't exist—only his hunger was real. In other words, instead of being able to logically see that Monica had been tending to their baby for hours upon hours and was rightfully dropping out, Leonard was mad that she was unable to empathize with him and jump up to help satisfy his immediate needs. There is absolutely no give-and-take.

People in these relationships might find themselves struggling to attract their partner's attention, to get them to listen to them or do anything that matters to them. This didn't become clear until Monica and Leonard's baby was born. It wasn't until there was something else pulling for her attention, which prevented her from giving Leonard 100 percent of her time, that she realized he was literally giving absolutely nothing to her. If whatever she wanted or needed didn't benefit Leonard, it wasn't happening. When she needed him, he didn't budge. She asked him to make dinner when she was truly exhausted, and he refused.

Monica finally described her relationship with Leonard this way: "It's as if I'm porous when I'm with him. His needs spill right through me. He's always calling the shots."

We have spent almost an entire book talking about how to move from a *me* to a *we*. Most people—especially if they want to—will be able to do this. But, as I said, Ultimate Controllers are not. They shut you down and shut you off. They tie you up in guilt and knots and leave you feeling helpless and frustrated, inept, and always angry.

The big question you might be kicking around is what I call the Over and Out Question: Is this relationship over and should I get out of it? This is a very personal decision, and there is no easy answer to it. But a clear indicator of it will be if you are often attempting to use the skills I taught you throughout this book and come up against constant refusal on the part of your partner— when there is no attempt to be a *we*. Time and time again your partner is on his own team, and there is an unwillingness to share. An Ultimate Controller will never play fairly.

When your partner is essentially unwilling to hear your feelings, then to stay in the marriage or relationship would mean continuing to surrender your identity and lose yourself. The only way to regain your sense of self and find the SelfNess we talked about is to finally leave the relationship. So in these cases, setting limits might mean actually getting out of the relationship.

Another warning sign is that you are always trying to reason with your partner, always trying to explain things to them with no reciprocity. Eventually, you completely lose your voice, give up and give in time and time again. Your partner always fails to recognize and relate to your feelings and emotions.

There were warning signs throughout Monica and Leonard's entire marriage. In fact, for most of their marriage, Monica prided herself on how little she asked of Leonard.

"If I asked nothing of him, what could be more valuable?" she asked me. "Look at this gift of devotion I have given him. How can he not love me for that?"

This seemed pretty normal to Monica. When she was nine years old her parents divorced. She still doesn't totally understand why; there was a lot of talk about "falling out of love." But once the initial whirlwind was over, she found that her mother was much sadder than she had been before. Monica had no time to think about herself. She spent the next nine years shuttling between houses, taking care of her mother when she was with her, and worrying about her when she wasn't. She made sure her mother ate and had something fun to do, and she attempted, as best she could, to make birthdays and holidays great. She would lie awake in bed when she was ten or eleven and try to figure out how she could get to the mall so she could buy her mother a birthday present—fully aware that it would be the only birthday present she would get.

When Monica and Leonard first met, they had what she thought was an amazing connection. How many people are lucky enough to experience that? He was handsome and articulate. He loved going to the movies with her. They had great sex. But what Monica didn't realize until she was in too deep was that he was completely nongiving.

Even from the beginning, every time Leonard got angry, it felt like he was going to walk out on the relationship, like the stakes were always high. When you are in a relationship with someone like Leonard, you feel like you are being possessed and you often confuse their controlling behavior toward you as love, as Monica did. Ultimate Controllers are very territorial, and they act like they own you. You can never please them, and you are constantly trying to figure out what you did wrong and how to change it. They have completely unreasonable and unrealistic expectations of you, so no matter how hard you try to meet them, you never will live up to them.

Monica was being dominated by Leonard on a regular basis. At first this arrangement worked for them. She truly didn't have strong opinions about the little things and was even happy to let him make most of the decisions. He basked in her attention, let her care for him, and made her feel special for doing it at first. They both had full-time jobs, but she did everything at home—cooked, cleaned, shopped, did the laundry. He, on the other hand, chose all the decorations and furniture. Again, that was a relief for her. She didn't care if they had a brown couch or a beige couch. Let him pick it, because it was easier that way. If he wanted steak for dinner, she got steak. She always made sure his side of the medicine cabinet was fully stocked with the things he wanted: Q-tips, lotion, deodorant. He didn't have to worry about a single detail. She wanted him to be happy.

And then they had the baby. And she no longer wanted to live in the city. The first true opinion she ever expressed. Sure, it was a doozy to decide where they would make their home. But he would hear none of it. There was no discussion.

"No way," he said harshly and definitively the first time she mentioned it. "I'm a city guy. I was born in the city, have always lived in the city, and it is in the city that we will live."

Monica was stunned.

"Can we at least talk about it?" she asked. "Make a list of the pros and cons?"

"If you want to live with me, you will have to live in the city," he said. "Here are your pros and cons: Pro, live with me. Con, live alone with the baby."

That was when she first realized she was in trouble. Not only did she have no negotiating power, but Leonard clearly didn't care one bit about what she thought or wanted.

Suddenly Monica started to see a different landscape that was not quite as idyllic as she first thought. Her life changed from wanting to do to having to do with a capital *H*. Leonard played with the baby when it suited him, but he never took on any of the tasks of cleaning or feeding or getting up in the night. And his demands on Monica increased.

Things got worse. One morning Leonard opened his side of the medicine cabinet looking for a Q-tip. He liked to clean out his ears every morning, it was part of his routine. The trouble was, the box was empty.

"Hey, where are the new Q-tips?" he called loudly into the bedroom where Monica was feeding the baby.

"Q-tips? We must be out," she said. "I've had a hard time getting to the store these days. I'll try to get some later."

"Later?" he said, coming to the door and staring harshly at her. "Later isn't good enough. My ears are going to bother me all day. I want you to get some now."

Monica looked down at the nursing baby and then up at Leonard.

"Here," Leonard boomed angrily. "Give me the baby. Go get the Q-tips. Fast! I have to leave in twenty minutes."

Monica started to feel like the soundtrack of her life—which used to be slow and pleasurable as she went through her daily tasks of pleasing Leonard, working and taking care of their home—had now sped up to an intolerable pace, which was neither pleasurable or even doable. Monica, who did not have a strong sense of self to begin with, was becoming completely invisible except as a means to meet the needs of Leonard and the baby.

The Q-tips incident played out over and over again when Monica forgot to pick up Leonard's shirts from the cleaners, or when they ran out of the soy sauce he had to have when they ate rice, or the time the baby had been sick for a week and Leonard opened his underwear drawer and found it empty. And every time Leonard was more angry than the time before. The incident in the bedroom over dinner, when she was trying so desperately to rest, might not have been a surprise after everything leading up to it, but it was the last straw. Monica realized she had to end her marriage, and we started to talk about this in my office. They tried counseling, but it didn't work, and Leonard refused to go back, which is typical of an Ultimate Controller who is generally unwilling and unable to change once confronted with their selfishness. So now that Monica was getting some of the caretaking duties that, to be perfectly honest, she required to be happy through nurturing her son, she was able to find the strength to stand up to Leonard and, eventually, leave the marriage for good.

Martyrs like Monica generally love to nurture, and they are good at it, but it becomes a serious question of balance, which is something I will talk more about in the next chapter. In her marriage, the balance was completely out of whack. It wasn't until she had her child and could feel fulfilled through that nurturing relationship that she truly realized what her husband was putting her through. She knew she could no longer take care of her child and her husband, because it would be like taking care of two kids.

As we've seen, Ultimate Controllers are so completely selfish that they lack the ability to empathize with other people. As you know, empathy, along with some of the other skills I talked about, is so, so important in a working relationship. But they simply can't begin to imagine what someone else is feeling, and they don't want to.

If your partner is an Ultimate Controller, it is always going to be about them, and you and your actions will never be good enough. You probably have a constant and high degree of guilt that goes along with your sense of responsibility toward that person. You take care of them to make their lives work, but because they are always dissatisfied, you will never succeed and will therefore end up feeling like a failure. You can never do enough to make them happy, so you feel bad about yourself because of it.

Really, it doesn't matter how much you've done. The Ultimate Controller lives by the adage, "What have you done for me lately?" He's me-centric and wears blinders to others' needs, feelings, and desires. Pete also eventually came to the same conclusion that Monica did; he would never be able to find happiness in his marriage. But it took him a long time to get there, and it was after he did much work to attempt to improve his relationship. His wife Julia made him very unhappy, but few would have guessed it from the outside. She was pretty and involved in the local social scene. But she was downright mean to Pete and was never ever satisfied with what he did for her.

He should have known. Whenever they were out with his friends, and the question about how they got together came up, Julia would say, "My friends just didn't get it. They always told me that Pete was not right for me, but I told them, 'You know what? I'm marrying potential.'"

As is typical of an Ultimate Controller, nothing Pete did ever measured up. Julia criticized him relentlessly and publicly, but only in front of his friends, never hers. No matter how much money he made, it was never enough for her. She would often disparage the great living he made and say to him, "You expect me to live on that?"

He could never live up to her expectations, and because he thought she was smart and trusted her opinion, he believed what she said.

"Do you know what Pete's annual bonus was this year?" she would ask his friends at the table. "A third of what it was last year!"

She even insulted him in front of their kids. She ridiculed him and constantly interrupted him with all the things he was doing wrong and all the things she "needed" him to do for her. When he was in the bathroom, she'd walk right in and bombard him with a catalog of complaints and a list of demands. Consequently he was jumpy and could never really relax anywhere in his own home.

When they went out to dinner, she would say she wasn't very hungry, that she would just have a salad, and then she would help herself to whatever was on Pete's plate and eat at least half of it. As far as she was concerned, his food was her food. Her sense of entitlement was so strong that, in fact, she saw everything as hers and felt she had the right to take whatever she wanted of his.

Food was often a problem for them. He regularly worked late, so when he got home he would ask Julia if she could make him something to eat, but she always refused. So he asked if the nanny could maybe start to leave him a plate. Again Julia said no, that wasn't in the nanny's job description. So he tried again, suggesting that Julia simply make a little extra of whatever she served the kids for dinner and leave that for him.

"Do you have any idea of what you are asking and how hard that is to do?" she asked.

So one night he headed toward the refrigerator to see what he could pull together for himself.

"That food is for the kids," she screeched as he chose some turkey and cheese to make a sandwich. Julia basically refused to feed him. He couldn't get nurtured on any level. So he started either eating out alone on his way home from work or picking up something and bringing it home with him.

Then there was the time he came home from work on a Friday evening after an especially hard week. He was so happy to be home and just relax. It was raining outside, and it felt cozy inside. As soon as he sat down she was on him.

"We have to go to the furniture store now," she said.

"Why now?" he asked. "I'm exhausted. I just want to stay home and unwind. I need some downtime."

"Your downtime was your commute home from work," she said. "We have to go now. I have to order the couch so it can be here in two weeks. Let's go."

"Can't we do it tomorrow?" Pete asked, turning on the television.

"We'll do it tonight," Julia said, taking the remote out of his hand and turning off the set he had just turned on. She obstructed any opportunity for his needs to be met. Pete had been through this so many times before, and he knew that she refused to take no for an answer. It just wasn't worth the fight. She harangued and bombarded and fought until, eventually, he gave in. He could either go and get it over with, or fight her and then eventually go anyway, because she would never leave him alone. For him, it became a choice of picking his poison.

The furniture shopping went downhill from there. When they got to the store, and Pete saw what Julia had chosen, he said he didn't like it.

"Yes, you do," she said, flatly negating his preference.

And then, to make matters worse, when it was delivered to their house two weeks later, Julia turned to him and said, "I chose that because you liked it so much." As I mentioned was typical of an Ultimate Controller, Julia denied Pete's reality. Whatever was going on with him just didn't exist in her world, and she always insisted that his choice was whatever she wanted for herself. There was no space for him to breathe.

One of Pete's issues was that he had a pronounced sense of responsibility toward his wife; he truly believed that it was up to him to make her happy. Despite her upsetting behavior, when he didn't make her happy, he felt tremendously guilty that he was falling short of being a good husband. So, as is typical, Pete, like Monica, went along with trying to make Julia's life work. But in Julia's Judgment Mirror he always could have and should have been doing more. If you are in a relationship with someone like Julia, you can never win. You can never do enough or give enough. You can never really please them, because they always want more.

Pete and Julia tried therapy several times, but whenever they reached the point when the therapist confronted Julia about considering her husband's needs, she would get angry and say the therapist was not good.

"She can't fix you," Julia would say to him. Then she would insist that they change therapists and declare to him, "You have to come with me. I know that I can fix you."

For a long time Pete believed he could make his marriage work, but each time Julia criticized him or berated him, he realized she killed a bit of love and respect that he had for her. He finally told her, "One day I will have nothing left for you." And she again completely ignored his words and refuted his feelings.

"That's not true," she told him. "That is not how you feel."

They were in the ultimate Selfish Showdown. She would not listen to him, acknowledge his issues, consider his feelings, and she certainly didn't empathize with him in any way. Finally he reached the point where he decided to end the marital therapy and continue on his own to sort out what was happening in his marriage. After he worked on his own issues, he realized he could not make his marriage work by himself. Julia was completely unwilling to compromise or reciprocate the effort he made.

The Ultimate Controller usually exhibits their behavior in one of two ways. Like Leonard, he can be aggressive and overt in his demands, or like Julia, she can be manipulative and down putting. Leonard was very vocal and always told Monica exactly what he wanted. In his mind there was no such thing as a joint decision. He took what he needed without ever thinking about how it would affect Monica, and without any discussion, he announced what they were going to do, where and what they were going to eat, where they would vacation, and which friends they would see.

Julia manipulated Pete by making him feel guilty when he didn't respond immediately to her demands, and she constantly made him feel terrible about himself. She had the ability to make him feel so awful that, at times, he actually thought he was the greedy and selfish one if he didn't cooperate immediately. She would dump a lot of her responsibility on to his shoulders by neglecting to tell him important details of their life (the car had been leaking oil and needed to be taken in immediately, but he would have to do it, because she had to go to work now or be late) and then say she had already told him about the problem, when she had not. In this way, he would be blindsided with more and more to do, without warning, and have a difficult time keeping up, no matter how hard he tried. The extra thorn that was always thrown in was that it was his fault because he didn't remember whatever it was that had to get done. Big or small, it always came down to Julia's blaming him and never taking responsibility for anything. In her reality, she was never wrong.

Of course you can experience similar bad feelings with Takers and Controllers; the difference here it that Ultimate Controllers look to reinforce your guilt and capitalize on your insecurities. When all is said and done, the Ultimate Controller won't be able to and simply doesn't want to be part of a team. So when Takers and Controllers are able to come around and play the Ace of Hearts Card or tune in to the Rules of Engagement, Ultimate Controllers won't. If you are in a relationship with an Ultimate Controller, they are not likely to change and that will eventually become clear.

Monica and Pete realized that they were not being heard on any level and got absolutely no consideration from their partners. Their partners could not and would not hear them. There was no way to play the Ace of Hearts Card for either of them. Their partners would not acknowledge or consider them, and they clearly had no empathy for them at all. Their partners shut down all attempts to engage in joint problem solving conversations or to work out a balance or a *we* in their conversations. Both their partners would always Bottom Line it: Leonard would get angry and threaten with leaving, and because Julia was relentless she would get angrier and louder until she overpowered him. Eventually both Monica and Pete made the decision that they were better off alone.

These examples, of course, are the extreme, because more often than not there is a way to achieve balance and communicate with each other in a loving, healthy, caring way.

Most of the couples who have struggled in one way or another throughout this book are making it work. They have put the tools in place, and they have found their way back to a loving relationship. They have learned to compromise and cooperate, and above all else, they truly care about what their partner needs and wants. If you are each thinking about the other, nobody will get lost and everyone will be fulfilled in one way or another. Read on and you'll see how they did it.

Chapter 8

We're in This Together

LYDIA HAD THE LENTILS SPREAD OUT ON PARCHMENT PAPER, ready to pick over them to make sure there were no stones. To be perfectly honest, it was the last thing she wanted to do. She should have decided to make hamburgers instead. She gathered a small handful and sifted through them just as the phone rang.

"Hey."

"Hey," Lydia answered, smiling at the sound of Jake's voice. She put the phone between her neck and her shoulder so she could keep sifting. She didn't want to lose too much time. She still had to chop the vegetables and then let everything simmer for a while.

"What are you up to?" Jake asked.

"Sifting, chopping, sautéing, the usual," Lydia said nicely, without any edge to her voice.

"Why don't we do something unusual?" Jake asked, and from the sound of his voice Lydia could tell he was smiling.

"Sure," she said. "What?"

"Why don't you go upstairs and get dressed. Let's go out to dinner."

Lydia hesitated for a brief second before the relief flooded through her.

"That sounds great," she said, putting the vegetables back in the refrigerator and deciding to deal with the lentils later—maybe tomorrow.

"I'll pick you up in a half hour."

When Jake came in to see me shortly after their evening out, he couldn't wait to tell me about it. He said he knew how hard Lydia worked to make dinner each night and was glad to be able to take the pressure off. And, he said, she was happy and appreciative. They had so much fun together. There was a lot to talk about and no fighting or blaming or tugging for each of their own needs.

"We talked like we did in the old days," he told me. "It was so easy. Not too long ago we would have fought the whole way to dinner about where to eat, what to eat, who should drive. There was none of that."

"You guys were already on the road to repair," I told him. "You had begun to do some important work. But now you're bridging the gap with your thoughtfulness. You're finally really thinking about Lydia. These gestures can go a long way."

I asked him if it felt like the old *we,* and he smiled. Over the last year or so he had repeatedly told me how much he missed that, their being able to just be together, read, watch television, choose a movie or a restaurant without a fight. They used to truly enjoy each other and have lots of great sex. That was what he wanted, and now, with the effort they each had made, that was what he was getting.

They came in together shortly after this, and Lydia confirmed what I already knew. She told me how grateful she was. His thoughtfulness meant the world to her. She, too, marveled at how smoothly that evening went. For so long she had been digging her heels in and refusing to give an inch. But lately it had been much easier to relax, and she rarely felt the need to create a power struggle. That night, Jake picked a restaurant that she loved. She felt considered and cared for, as though they were in it together, so she didn't have to fight for herself. In fact, she was able to stop worrying about her own needs being met, because he was doing just that, and she started thinking about Jake's needs again.

This sort of thing is now becoming routine in Lydia and Jake's marriage. Each week she comes in with a story about how he did this or she did that. And I have never seen her smile as much as she has been lately. They are even talking about trying to have a baby.

Checks and Balances

I have been talking about the importance of moving from a *me* to a *we* for some time now, but what exactly does that look like? It is all about putting Checks and Balances in place that encourage you to limit your self needs to balance your needs as a couple. Being with and sharing with your partner should become as important as doing the things you want to do for yourself. The overriding notion and the question you should be asking is, What works for us?

When you answer this question together and implement the ideas you have agreed upon, you arrive at what I call Mutuality: the recognition that you are on the same side. You achieve a new balance between the time you each need to be your own person and do your jobs and follow your interests and hobbies with the time you share together so that you each feel special and important and number one in each other's lives. You figure out a way to make each other's needs important without sacrificing your individual needs, and you find a middle ground so that each of you feels your needs are, at the very least, acknowledged and addressed. The idea is that everything is reciprocal in some way; it is the give-and-take that flows between you when you know that you are both invested in your relationship and that there is something in it for each of you.

This brings me to the importance of compromise, which is the cornerstone of the *we* and the means by which you achieve Mutuality. It is what enables you to put those Checks and Balances in place because it makes room for everybody's needs. We can't have everything we want all the time, but at least having your partner acknowledge and understand your needs can really help you accept not always getting your own way. The art of compromising includes cooperating and problem solving as you move toward your new balance.

This system of Checks and Balances that I keep referring to is twofold. The first part of it is truly finding that middle ground where the *me* isn't lost and the *we* is strong for each couple. As I mentioned, there has to be space in every relationship for each

WE'RE IN THIS TOGETHER

person to shine. Everybody must be allowed to explore their interests, and as I said from almost page 1 of this book, it is nearly impossible that two halves of a couple will have all of the same interests. Therefore, there will always be those times when you will need or want to do things separately. But there must also be a big effort made to build togetherness time, as I mentioned, so that each partner feels appreciated and loved and important in the other's life.

Many people come into a relationship caught up in their own lives and their own needs. We saw this with Alyssa and Kevin as they struggled to find the middle ground I am talking about. You might remember that she was always ready to take the next step in their relationship long before he was, including saying I love you and moving in together. She knew she loved him and was ready to take the leap. He was happy with the way things were and, for a number of reasons, was more than hesitant to take any big steps. If things were going to work between them—as they have, I am happy to say—they had to shift from a me-centric frame of mind to a we-centric way of thinking. And that is exactly what they have done, but it took some hard work, more time than Alyssa would have preferred, and trust in each other to reach the point where they are now: getting engaged. In the end, Alyssa was patient and gave Kevin the time he needed, without limiting him. She let him know she wanted a future with him, but she never threatened to leave. In turn, he was always open with her, sharing his fears and telling her he did want her in his life. He talked about his anxieties and realized, because he loved her so much, that he didn't want to take the chance of losing her. He went into therapy to work through the cold feet that were preventing him from moving forward. Instead of letting his fears continue to hold him back, he held on to the fact that he loved being with her and followed his heart. He moved beyond his comfort zone and his *me* to make room for the *we* with a marriage proposal.

Tina and Jerome were also finally able to strengthen their *we*. Do you remember how he took over everything in their lives, including how they decorated their home? Once he was finally able to play the Ace of Hearts Card and acknowledge what he was doing and then truly consider how his behavior was making her feel so bad—that Tina had no room to hang a single picture she wanted up in their house—he was able to empathize and began to make changes. He took down two of his Yankees prints and made space for her to finally hang her family pictures that she had been wanting to put up for so long. This was a big step for them and the first toward sharing their home space together.

The other part of this equation of Checks and Balances is making sure that the shared responsibility between you is as even and fair as it can be. Do you remember Tabitha and Levi? They suffered from the "No Fair" Paper Cut. Each felt taken advantage of and burdened. They are both professors who teach full course loads and oversee graduate students. They also have two young boys who are constantly going to one activity or another. Tabitha and Levi found themselves fighting all the time about the fact that they each thought they carried a heavier load. What I teach my patients to do is to shift from always thinking about what *I* do versus what *you* do to how can I help you and how can you help me. This goes back to so many of the skills we have already learned: asking for help when you need it, asking nicely, and pulling out the Ace of Hearts Card. And now, the Checks and Balances.

Instead of each feeling constantly overburdened and like they were in the struggle alone, one option for Tabitha and Levi might be to make the decision that if one partner makes dinner, the other will do the dishes and vice versa. If one partner does the laundry all week, the other is responsible for picking up the cleaning. Whatever it is you have to get done in your lives over the course of a week, do what you can to not only equalize the load but also to allow each of you to know what to expect and what you are expected to do. And when you work out this system, make sure it works for both of you and capitalizes on each of your strengths, weaknesses, and preferences. If you are a good house cleaner and your husband is awful at it, maybe that should land on your to-do list. You can then balance it out with what you don't like doing, for example, lawn work. Or say you are a great cook but he isn't, well, then that can be your job, but maybe the food shopping will fall to him. This is where sharing a cooperative spirit comes into play and becomes so important. It helps create the partnership between the two of you that allows you to maximize and pool the strengths you each have for the good of the couple, thereby becoming stronger than ever and having more power to get done what needs to get done.

If you know your partner is working hard at certain things to make your life together run smoothly, it eases the weight of all the responsibility you carry, taking a lot of pressure off of you and allowing you to relax. We saw this with Lydia and Jake. He no longer wants the burden of dinner to fall on her exclusively, and this has helped her feel less resentful about the times it does. Similarly, Tabitha and Levi are now working on a new arrangement. On the days he takes the boys to their activities, she cooks dinner and vice versa. On the days they are both so busy neither has an inch, they order a pizza or make a sandwich, and there are no hard feelings. They each put the boys to bed every other night so there is no discussion about it. And they have decided to leave most of the housework for the weekends, when they spend one of the mornings sharing that burden. Tabitha and Levi now know what they each must do and what is expected of them, and there are no questions or festering anger because they no longer have to wait for the other to pick up the slack.

The Winning Team

Another important piece of information I tell my patients over and over again is to Stop Keeping Score. Stop paying attention to who fed the children breakfast all week or who took the dog for a walk more mornings. Here is the secret to that: It all comes out in the wash! Sure, tonight you might do more. You might make dinner, do the dishes, *and* put the kids to sleep while he is working late. But maybe next week you'll have the chance to go out with a friend, and he'll do all of these things. Over time, when you are working as a team, it will even out. It might not be the case that everything will be equal on a concrete level, though.

You might, in fact, put the kids to bed more than he does. But it will equal out emotionally, because he will give back in other ways. There will be situations and times when he carries a heavier burden, and there will be times you do. And there are probably certain things you do and certain things he does. You might find it very annoying that you *always* scoop the cat's litter box and restock the house with toilet paper. He never even thinks about it! But what are the things that he *always* does? Deal with the upkeep of the car and paying the bills? And do you give those chores any thought? As I said, it can all equal out. Keeping score will simply keep you in that selfish frame of mind and prevent the *we* from shining through. Knowing that everything will equal out in one way or another will allow you to move from No Fair to Fair Play.

The reality is that there is so much to do for everyone that nobody can really keep up. Everyone is juggling more than their fair share, so you just have to decide jointly to get through it together and accept that there will be days you do more and there will be days he does more. If you trust that your partner has your back and is not out to get you, and that if you need help he will give it to you, it lightens your load. Look at the big picture instead of measuring each dinner and each bedtime routine and every time the dog has to be taken out. Tabitha and Levi have been able to do this by no longer fighting over each menial job. Their goal as a team is to take care of their family and their house while each is able to be successful at the university. They are making that happen together.

Do you remember what threw Tabitha over the edge and forced her to begin to make these changes with Levi? It was that pipe that burst in the powder room. She became so angry at that point that she was the one who was always stuck with the unexpected burden, having to find a substitute to teach her classes and cancel her appointments with students, that she knew she had to make some changes. When she told me about the pipe, I told her about that always looming Wild Card I talked about in chapter 6: when the unexpected occurs. There are so many Wild Cards that can, at any moment, come into play from illness to a lost wallet, creating an imbalance in your already unbalanced life. When Tabitha thought of the burst pipe as a Wild Card, a single situation gone awry, rather than as proof that she was always stuck handling more at home, she began to see things in perspective. She could now identify the Wild Cards in the bigger picture and could see that her rearranging her day to take care of them was sometimes a matter of practicality. She became less resentful about these unexpected occurrences as well as their daily tasks. She realized that working with Levi as a team gave them strength and fortitude to deal with these Wild Cards and anything else that came along and make it through. Maybe next time, he could handle the slack from the Wild Card, but without him, she would miss out on the idea that they are in it together as well as the strength that comes from sharing the burden. This Wild Card can come up and perpetuate any Selfish Hot Spot, so try to be aware of it and separate it from your other everyday occurrences.

Slowly, between coming up with a system that worked for their daily lives as well as identifying when Wild Cards come into play, Tabitha and Levi were able to really start to work as a *we*.

As Jake did with Lydia, Levi was able to begin to think beyond his own needs and start thinking about hers. He began to let her sleep late on Sunday mornings while he took the kids to the park and out for breakfast. This led her to think about what she could do to make his life easier and more pleasurable. Because they stopped keeping score, were aware of the Wild Cards, and started using their Checks and Balances system, their family life became enjoyable again.

Playing Your Cards Right

With the right cards in place—including your Ace of Hearts Card, knowing not to let the Wild Card throw you out of whack, and other gambits like a we-centric mind frame, Mutuality, compromise and cooperation, and Checks and Balances—you will now be able to get to the nitty-gritty: problem solving, which is when you are literally working together to solve a problem. This is the heart and soul of sharing. As you did before, ask the question, How can we make this work for both of us?

It will help to know that some changes you might have to make to solve your problems will be necessary. For example, one of the most challenging aspects of getting married is that it becomes necessary to shift some of the boundaries of your life from your family of origin to your new family. You must begin to prioritize the time you spend with your partner so that they feel important. Because people are so used to being a part of their own family, what many people try to do is simply make their spouse an extended member of the family. That way, in theory, not much would have to change. But it just doesn't work that way. Everything has to be anchored to the idea that you and your husband now are a family unto itself. This is very hard to do, but understanding that it is the normal flow of things might help.

This did not happen easily for Sofia and Scott. Scott is the Super Sibling who, following his parents' lead, did everything for his sister Hazel. For example, remember how Sofia and Scott would wait around every weekend to see when Hazel was available and Sofia was so upset about it? They could never make advanced plans of their own. I explained all of this to Sofia and Scott about the family and assured Scott that each partner, of course, must be able to find time to be with their own family. The equation, though, must shift so that the emphasis is on the couple and the *we* is preserved and nurtured. I helped him understand that this prioritizing was necessary in order to move to their compromise. Sofia had to come first. He had to make her feel special, and he needed to consider her and talk to her before unilaterally agreeing to anything. They had to work out a system as a couple—a compromise—that worked for both of them.

Problem solving simply means being able to work together as a team, to explore all the options that are available and that each person prefers, and then come to a common agreement that works for both people. After many fights and then a few calmer discussions, Scott finally understood that the time he spent with Hazel was greatly taking away from his new life. He slowly made a shift away from the emotional responsibility he felt toward his sister and his parents and started to put limits in place. For example, he said he would still like to have brunch with his family on the weekends, but if they were not able to choose a day by Wednesday, then he and Sofia would make their own plans. If it worked out that they were still free on the day the family chose to get together, then great, they would go. If not, they would try again the next weekend.

Tess and Pablo also had to work together to find a system that worked for them. One of their differences that helped to bring them together in the first place—their openness to each other's different religions—was what was blocking them now. Initially Tess had agreed to raise their girls in Pablo's religion—Catholic— but after finding comfort in her own religion—Judaism—after her sister's death, she began to rethink their plan. The rift caused a great strain on their marriage, but they are now able to both understand that marriage is dynamic and ever-changing in the same way life is, so they have to be open to changing with it. Pablo understands now that when Tess agreed to raise their girls Catholic, she meant it. She couldn't foresee what would happen and how that might shift her feelings. She, too, has been able to find value again in Pablo's strong religious beliefs. They are finally able to see their differences as a positive again.

Using her Heart Talk, Tess has been able to help Pablo understand that her reconnection to Judaism has helped her feel connected to her sister and to sever that now would be devastating. At the same time, she was able to relate to his sense of disappointment. With all of that in mind they have been able to come up with a plan. The girls will continue to be raised Catholic, but Pablo is now willing to make room in their lives to explore Judaism through some of the traditions and holidays.

It is so important in a marriage to understand that life and circumstances change, and each partner must be willing to be flexible and grow through these transitions in order to maintain a strong and healthy relationship.

That has been hard for Emily and Ned since Ned lost his job. But after using the tools in the book, Emily has become more understanding of what Ned is going through. Instead of seeing his job loss as what it is taking away from her, she stopped blaming him and became supportive and helpful in his quest for a new job. Because she was able to empathize with him, he was able to respond to her needs in a new way. He heard her concerns about his not wearing clean clothes and, even though he was feeling bad, made the effort to look nice and change his shirt. They are now able to deal with the loss of his job as a shared issue, not just his problem.

Let's look at how Marcie and Josh are doing in their dealing with a similar issue. As you know, for years she has thought Josh pays more attention to his BlackBerry than he does to her. Can you imagine what happened when he decided to take up community theater and actually got the lead in *Annie Get Your Gun*? Marcie went crazy. Suddenly she was fighting against a double-header: his BlackBerry and his sudden love and commitment to the theater. She was completely jealous and felt her position in his life had dropped to number three. Now, while it is of course vital for Josh to have his *me* time, he also needs to find a way to include Marcie in his days. They have to work out a compromise to find a balance between the *me* and the *we*. Josh needs to consider how his choices are taking time away and making an impact on their *we*, and he needs to speak to it and be willing to compromise in order to find a balance.

They began to problem solve. First, he suggested she come to the performances, but she countered that then she feels like just another audience member, not like she is sharing something special with him. He told her he was upset by that, because he wanted her to be excited about his lead role.

"I want you to see me acting," he told her.

"Of course I'll come to a performance," she said. "It's really the rehearsals that bother me. You're out all the time! We barely spend any time together anymore. You're rehearsing on Saturdays *and* Sundays."

"What would you like me to do?" he asked.

She thought for a minute. "I'd like to have one full weekend day with you," she said. "They can't expect you to donate your entire life to the production. Can you talk to someone and ask if they can have you rehearse on only one weekend day for longer instead of a few hours here and there, which then creeps into our entire weekend?"

"Sure, I'll talk to the director," he finally conceded. "I'll make sure we have some solid weekend time together each week."

"Thank you," she said.

Josh followed through, agreeing to rehearse all day on Saturdays—so he got home in time for dinner—and then not at all on Sundays. He started to plan picnics and hikes that they both liked to do. Once Marcie started to feel included in his life again, she became more accepting of his acting. She found herself asking about his character and even offering to run lines with him. He was thrilled and then wanted to do something for her. He suggested they take a vacation together, and he told her he would try out for only two of the four plays each year—a third only if it was a great play. She was happy with that. They were finally consciously carving out the *we* time that had gotten lost.

Let's not forget about the BlackBerry. Finally, after much discussion and heartache, Josh came to see that his anxiety over his job—which led to his constant BlackBerry use—was taking over his life, and he had to put a stop to that too. He couldn't let it continue to disrupt his marriage.

He had every right to expect Marcie to be supportive and understanding of his anxiety, but he was finally aware of the damage it was doing and wanted to prevent it from spilling into their *we* time. He became much better at managing it. Consequently, Marcie was able to stop pushing against him and stop seeing the BlackBerry as her enemy. Instead of fighting the BlackBerry and constantly accusing him of doing something wrong, she became more reassuring and understood that the BlackBerry was a symbol of Josh's stress, not of his choice to be away from her. Once Marcie became more tolerant and less angry, they were able to move toward concrete problem solving.

"If your BlackBerry isn't on constantly when you're home, it might not be so distracting, and I would be a lot happier," she told him.

Josh started to turn off his BlackBerry before dinner and checked in only one more time before he went to bed. That way he could deal with any pressing issues before he entered the bedroom. This calmed him down and allowed them to resume having sex at night, which is what she wanted to do all along. And because her needs were being met, she was able to start thinking about his. One morning recently, Marcie reached across the bed and felt how excited he was. He responded immediately, getting turned on, and the first thing he did was make sure his BlackBerry was turned off.

Trent and Violet had a similar issue that they were finally able to work through. Do you remember Trent? He came home after work and played Guitar Hero, because he felt he needed it after his busy days. But Violet did not understand that. She wanted to be with him from the moment he walked in the door. They found a resolution by deciding that Trent could play video games guilt-free and uninterrupted for twenty minutes when he walked in the door. He would go right to the den and start to play. Violet knew, of course, that he came home, and she timed it, but in her mind she pretended that it was still part of his workday. Sometimes she would do her own activity in the den while he played, but she never bothered him. And then, when twenty minutes were up, he felt better and they greeted each other like he had just walked in the door. That was when they began their evenings together. Because Trent was able to decompress, he felt both relieved and supported by her, and consequently he was able to be genuinely and positively involved with her.

One important thing to keep in mind is that there are different ways for couples to share time. People want to spend time together, and that can mean a shared activity such as taking a walk together or, of course, having sex, or there might be times when you are in the same room, literally sharing space and time, but you are doing your own activities. You have to carve out that quality time, as Marcie and Josh did, but you also have to continue to make room for your own and your partner's interests.

Back to Bed

Compromising outside of the bedroom can actually lead you into the bedroom. So many people who were struggling have now found a way to be happy there.

Jenna was so angry with Gabe, because she felt controlled by him in so many corners of their lives, especially in their sex life. When this happens, people often respond in a tit-for-tat manner, each retaliating for what they believe their partner did to hurt them. And this only serves to perpetuate the problem, and the divide between them grows wider. It can start outside the bedroom with any Selfish Hot Spot—he never does the dishes, she can't be bothered to take her garbage out of the car—and then follow them into the bedroom as one or the other begins to withhold sex to get back at the other. Tit for tat is a negative attempt to even the score. When Gabe didn't get what he wanted, he became angry, and his anger turned Jenna off and made their sexual connection almost nonexistent. You know, it's the same old story: she didn't want to have sex, he got mad, then she didn't want to have sex because he was so mad, and he just got angrier. This is the typical sexual standoff and power struggle that so many people reach. It can happen anywhere but often flares up in the bedroom because people are less inclined to talk about sexual disappointments, so they communicate by trying to get even. For Lydia and Jake, when he stopped romancing her, they got to this point. It may appear differently for different couples, but so many people who find themselves not having sex may be caught up in this common Selfish Standoff over who is initiating sex and how often it is happening.

Remember in chapter 4 when Jenna asked me, "Do I *have* to have sex with him?" I told her that having sex with your husband is part of your marriage bond and commitment to each other: to share intimacy together. Somehow her sexual esteem and desire to have sex had gotten lost because she felt it was sex on demand. She needed to speak up and assert herself about when she wanted to have sex and when she didn't so that, instead of withdrawing in anger, she could meet her husband's needs as well as her own. As I mentioned, time and time again when there are emotional problems between people, their sexual life can go down the drain.

I explained to Jenna the importance of her SelfNess and her Sexual Esteem and, in this case, going from a *me* to a *we* meant owning and holding on to her sexual esteem so she could share it with Gabe. She had to stop letting it become a factor in the tit for tat and using it as a bargaining chip. I talked to her about being able to reconnect to her own sexual desire, which would be the first step toward recapturing their sexual connection. Sex is a physical way to express emotional love. In order to get back to those positive feelings she used to have, she had to find her way back to her own sexual desire and build up her Sexual Esteem. Then having sex with Gabe would be her choice because, presumably, she would want to.

I told her, and I will tell you too, that it is important for couples to have a sexual connection. This is something worth working toward maintaining. The answer to alleviating the power struggles that take place is to choose to be involved, make the choice to do something for your partner, rather than feel forced into it. Once you make it your decision and personal desire to be with your partner, it will help you sidestep the Selfish Standoff and stop you from giving up your own pleasure in retaliation.

As I mentioned in chapter 5, Jenna started to regain her voice first outside the bedroom. She began to express herself to Gabe and became much stronger through the work we did in therapy. She started to ask for what she needed and find her SelfNess. And then they played the Ace of Hearts Card, first resolving their emotional issue about her not moving to Texas to be near his family, which was the big issue that loomed over them always.

"I know you've been upset about our not moving, and I am so sorry about that," she told him. "But when you isolate yourself when we're with my family, it's hurtful. I understand that you miss your family, but I would really appreciate it if you could spend time with us when we are all together."

And then they were able to talk about their lack of sexual intimacy, "And I understand that you want to have sex more often," she said. "I want to have sex with you, but I don't want to all the time. I'm okay with once a week."

"That doesn't seem like enough to me," Gabe said honestly. "I really want it more."

"Well, can we at least try it and start there?" she asked. "Wouldn't once a week be better than never? We haven't had sex in a while."

He had to admit she made sense. "Yes," he finally said. "Once a week would be better than the way it has been lately."

So she successfully negotiated a compromise for herself with him. She promised to make love once a week, with the caveat that she could say no on a given night as long as she told him which night that week they would be together. She was hitting her sexual hold button. He actually listened to her. He stopped demanding sex and started to consider when she would be in the mood. He asked her now and paid attention to her cues. He became more tolerant when she didn't want to, because they were able to talk about when they would be together. Now he could look forward to being with her instead of lying in bed and feeling rejected and furious, wondering if and when they would have sex again. By Jenna's reassuring him that she wanted to be with him and that when she didn't want to have sex, it was not because of him, he was able to stop feeling so angry and insecure. Instead, he felt loved. And she found that, with the pressure off, she actually enjoyed having sex with Gabe. Eventually, they recaptured their sexual intimacy. They reached a sexual compromise: he didn't ask to have sex all the time as he used to, and she said yes more often and meant it.

Different Strokes for Different Folks

And while so much emotional energy creeps into the sexual connection, there are, as we have seen, times when the sexual act itself
is enough to cause a rift. This can happen when people are dealing
with differences in tastes and preferences. Compromising in the
bedroom is crucial, because if you don't, your sex life itself will
be compromised. Even more important, so much of the positive
energy that flows between you and your partner comes from that
honest desire to please your partner and their desire to please you.

You remember Neil and Mary Beth and Henry and Gail? They
are slowly working out their sexual problems, and it is because
they have finally come to accept that they don't want the same
things, they don't even like many of the same things, but they
love each other. Because they have used their Heart Talk and are
past their anger, they are now willing and able to learn how to
compromise. Before, they were often unwilling to give in to their
partner's needs, because it felt like sacrificing their own desires
and surrendering to what their partner wanted, without any room
for what they liked. But now, because they have changed the way
they think and talk about it, pleasing their partner has become
synonymous with pleasing themselves. Now they are both invested
in their sex life.

For Henry and Gail the issue was birth control, which, when
an agreement couldn't be reached, shut down the activity in their
bedroom. Gail decided she didn't want to take the pill anymore;
she was tired of putting hormones into her body. And Henry

hated using condoms; he would rather not have sex then use one. So they stopped having sex, and they both lost out. Because there was no *we,* they had no team. It finally reached the point where they were so disappointed about missing out on having sex together that they began by playing the Ace of Hearts Card: they each acknowledged the other's preference.

"I know you don't want to take the pill," Henry said to Gail. "I understand that you don't want to put your body in any harm, and I don't want you to either. But there are other options out there. There is the diaphragm, the sponge, IUDs. Would you be willing to explore any of those options? We could do it together. We can play around, see how each one feels."

"Why can't you just use a condom?" Gail asked.

"I'd be willing to use condoms on occasion, but not all the time," he answered. "Can't we please try some of the other options? If you choose one and you don't feel like using it all the time, I'll trade off with you. Sometimes you can use the birth control and sometimes I can. What do you say?"

Gail finally agreed. It made sense to her. It was a real compromise. They each gave something and they each received something. And the reason they were able to come to this agreement was because each finally realized that this was about individual preferences and desires. It was not a personal attack against the other person or a rejection of them. Just as Marcie was finally able to work with Josh's choices about his BlackBerry and joining the local theater group, understanding this can ease the hurt, pain, and disappointment people feel. It will help ease so much of that annoying Selfish Hot Spot behavior that people take so personally. The real goal is to learn how to be tolerant of those annoying behaviors to the point where you don't experience them as a deliberate declaration of not loving you. As I mentioned with Jenna, it is so important that your partner can reassure you that they are not doing it on purpose. It is not an attack on you in any way, and they are willing to work on managing it so it is not so disruptive. And when it is necessary, you can reassure your partner of the same things. This helps each person feel loved and secure and makes the disagreement, and sometimes the disappointment that comes along with it, much easier to accept. Henry has to understand that Gail's not wanting to take the pill is not a personal affront to him and has nothing to do with her wanting to have sex with him. It is a separate issue. So once he understands that, and she understands that his not wanting to use condoms is also not directed at her personally, then they can work to accept each other's preferences. With that accomplished they can move forward.

Neil and Mary Beth have another difference in preferences: he loves blow jobs and would love to get one several times a week; she hates them and would like to never give them. What are they supposed to do? I suggested an alternative that would respect her discomfort but at the same time leave room for his pleasure. Why doesn't she simply close her eyes and lick him like a lollipop instead of putting his whole penis in her mouth, which was what she hated? After doing that for a while, she could use her hands, which he liked almost as much as the real thing. That sounded good to both of them. And even this was agreed to be done on a limited schedule: on special occasions and once a month when he asks her to. Although it was understood that she always had the option of saying no and that she would prefer to do it another night. It was enough of a compromise for both of them. She stopped dreading sex because she knew she wouldn't be forced to do something she hated, and he continued to look forward to it because he knew he would get a little treat every once in a while.

Neil was finally able to see that her hating to give blow jobs was not a rejection of him or his penis, and he had learned to not take it personally and was able to accept her preferences. And his wanting blow jobs had nothing to do with his not caring about asking her to do something she didn't like. He just really enjoyed them.

"I understand that it is a turn-off for you," he said to her. "But it is a turn-on for me."

She was finally able to feel good about making him feel good. They are in this together, finally, as a *we*. And sometimes lately, because she now truly sees the delight in pleasing him and because it has now become her choice, she even surprises him with a full, old-fashioned blow job.

Florence and Rafael were able to come to a similar agreement and understanding around the same issue: she loves oral sex and he doesn't. Using their Heart Talk they talked through it and, just as Neil did, Florence realized that Rafael's reluctance had nothing to do with her. It was his own personal preference. And at the same time, because he saw how much oral sex meant to her, he stopped experiencing it as her being thoughtless of him.

When it comes to sexual preferences and taste, the art of compromise often revolves around how often it's going to happen. So while something that one partner enjoys but the other doesn't won't be the main staple of your sex life, it doesn't have to be totally absent or off-limits. It can be treated as a special occasion activity, such as a birthday, an anniversary, or any cause for celebration. That way, everyone's needs are understood and met. Consider it a love gesture, and it will make all the difference in the world.

Loretta and Sid also had different tastes in the bedroom. She wanted foreplay, and Sid wanted to get on with things. It wasn't that he was uncaring; the truth is, he got excited very quickly, and in his eyes he thought the sex they shared was great. But Loretta was often left cold and unsatisfied. By using Heart Talk, she was finally able to share her needs with Sid in a positive and caring way, telling him what she liked and didn't like. Because he wasn't feeling blamed or criticized as a bad lover, he was finally able to hear her and factor in her needs.

Let's peek in at Crystal and Allen. Do you remember how lying in bed and waiting for Allen to join her and initiate sex would tie her up in knots? He would take his time, way too much time as far as she was concerned. She would lie there feeling unwanted because he was closing up the house and doing everything he needed to do before coming to bed to be with her. And it felt very personal. Understanding and accepting that they both have different styles—she could leave things for the morning but he could not—helped them each see that it wasn't personal.

They have decided that, instead of subtly heading off to bed and waiting, Crystal should talk about it. Now she actually asks him how long he will be. And he answers honestly. So she no longer feels like she is wasting her time waiting for him or that he isn't coming because he doesn't want to. He lets her know that he is looking forward to it. Sometimes she fits a bubble bath in during the half hour he is checking email and locking up for the night. They have each become both accepting and reassuring. When they finally meet in bed, everyone is happy to be there.

You probably remember that initiating sex was a huge issue for Charlotte and Reed. She felt like she did everything around the house and the least he could do was take on the task of initiating their sexual encounters. But Reed felt so much pressure he began to worry about losing his erection and stopped initiating at all, which made Charlotte livid. For them it came down to the fact that things were lopsided: there was too much on her and consequently she was putting too much on him. But it is not a fair expectation for one partner to have to initiate sex all the time. Not only is it too much responsibility in a relationship, but it left no room for Charlotte to express her own sexual desire. What they were finally able to do was share both loads of work in the house and in the bedroom. When Reed started to help with the cleaning and food shopping, he was able to bring more of the *we* to their daily lives and eliminate the *me*. Once Charlotte felt less burdened, she agreed that she would occasionally initiate sex.

The acceptance and understanding that Crystal and Allen and Charlotte and Reed found is really the key to moving forward together. We've seen it with all the couples who have succeeded in coming together as a team. And it is what ultimately brought many of the other couples we met in the earlier chapters of this book to find their *we* again. Each person was able to stop taking the other's behavior personally—this is so important—and to instead see it as an individual need or style. It was not a statement about one's feelings or lack of them for the other. Once that is determined, it is much easier for each person to find a way to manage the differences and work together.

Securing Your Right

I have been talking all along about the importance of moving from a *me* versus *you* stance to simply having a right to make room for your needs. Once most of the couples in this book were able to make that shift—to stop judging who was in the right and who wasn't and appreciate that each had a separate right of their own—they were able to stop competing and team up to find a compromise together. Let's check in on a few of the couples we've met along the way.

Chloe and Abe were able finally to accept that the way they each deal with family is different. Abe thinks extended family should be kept at a distance, but Chloe wanted her mother to stay with them after her mother was released from the hospital. Chloe can now see that Abe's choice has nothing to do with her or her mother. It is not because he doesn't like Chloe's mother that he does not want her to live with them. He simply needs his own space, and that is how he was brought up. And Abe is able to now see that Chloe's wanting her mother there has nothing to do with disregarding Abe's needs or not wanting to be alone with him. It is simply what Chloe thinks is the right thing to do. In the end, they made a compromise. Chloe's mom came to live with them for two weeks after she was released from the hospital, and then Chloe went to her house to take care of her for one week after that.

Sharon and Victor were able to finally accept that their planning styles were simply different—neither good nor bad—and that each one has nothing to do with the other. You might remember that Sharon liked to plan everything, and Victor did things on the spur of the moment and was often willing to change plans if something better came up or his family was involved. Once they reached this important level of acceptance, and each reassured the other that the choices they made in this regard were never meant to hurt the other, they were able to finally work together as a team. They placed a large calendar on their kitchen wall and worked together to make plans and talk about changing them when it was necessary.

Simply put, it so often comes down to timing. This was so true for Spencer and Brooke. She interrupted him all the time and he hated it. It became their Never-Ending Fight, because every time he was unavailable, her red flag would go up, and every time she interrupted him, trying to claim the time she thought was rightfully hers, his red flag would go up. But it was important for each of them to balance their *me* time with their *we* time. He deserved to have some time to himself, of course, but she deserved to have his attention at other times. What they did was carve out time that was meant for only them, which she was then able to look forward to. When she has the urge to interrupt him these days, she simply reminds herself that they have a walk planned at a specific hour. She can wait until then. And Spencer is finding that the time they spend together now is great, because it isn't forced upon him or preceded by an interruption.

In a more symbolic way, Maeve and Simon must also make time for each other. They still haven't reached a final conclusion about having a baby: she wants to, but he does not, since he feels caught up in taking care of his son from a previous marriage. But they are no longer fighting about it constantly. She has agreed to give him time free of constant badgering, and he has agreed to make some time to consider her. Together they decided that they will revisit the discussion in six months. By then Simon's son might be more settled. His concerns about having another baby have not gone away, but he is willing to remain open because he doesn't want to disappoint Maeve. The important thing here is Simon's willingness to keep the option alive and open.

And of course you remember Veronica, Sadie, and Maya who all gave up way too much of themselves and their time in one way or another to please their partners and to make their relationships work. Maya is finally learning to use her anger to bring about a change and not always let Walker off the hook, rather than accepting an apology too quickly like she always used to. Sadie went back to the gym and has no problem now telling Jonathan if she can't pick up an order or deal with an invoice because she doesn't want to miss her yoga class. She feels so much better about herself, and that resonates through their entire relationship.

Veronica has been able to consider her needs and make them known to Reuben. She wouldn't take no for an answer and finally got the tickets she has long wanted for a season of the local orchestra. She could finally hear the notes to her own music and got him to share that with her. By considering herself, they were able to build on it, and he began considering her as well.

They have all learned to embrace SelfNess and have started to reclaim themselves, which, in turn, has strengthened their marriages. They have learned to make sure they are nurtured individually as well as together. Each has begun to negotiate her needs within her relationship. They can now see their partnerships as a team effort rather than simply feeling like the batboys who do all the running around.

This is exactly what Monica and Pete were unable to do with their spouses, to form a team, that all-important element that can make a marriage or relationship so much smoother. It is something that couples too often lose sight of: that they are supposed to have the same general goals. Once you stop feeling pitted against each other, but rather that you are truly working together, then each thing your partner wants to do that doesn't include you, and the things you need to do for yourself that might not include him, don't seem so threatening. If the goal is to nurture your love, then, as I mentioned earlier, you have to be strong in yourself first, which then enables you to be strong as a couple.

Love You, Mean It!

The last skill to keep in mind as you move forward toward happiness is to do your best to Accentuate the Positive and build on the Love You, Mean It moments. In other words, focus on the good things your partner does that make you happy. If you are seething because your husband forgot to make the kids' lunches the night before, but he did make them a great breakfast and got them to school on time, focus on that. Balance your Hate You, Mean It moments with your Love You, Mean It moments. Jake's attempts to please Lydia made it easier for her to accept anything Jake did that she didn't like, which softened her anger and allowed all the positive, loving feelings to flow.

If you have begun to use the heart-talk skills that you learned in chapter 6, then you are finally on the road to rekindling your desire to make your partner happy. This means making choices that might please your partner, rather than continuing to let your anger get in the way and create that sexual and emotional disconnect you have been having. This helps to diminish the selfish behavior on both sides as you are both more sensitive and begin to respond to each other's needs so you can work on compromising.

Jake now finds pleasure in figuring out ways to lessen Lydia's load. The other day, the mail carrier mistakenly left a package that was not for them at their door. Before, Jake wouldn't have given it any thought. He would have simply left it in their foyer, knowing that Lydia would eventually deal with it. But this time he put it in the car and drove it back to the post office. And he picked up Lydia's favorite sandwiches for lunch on the way home. Lydia is thinking about ways to make Jake happy too. She wants to make sure Jake doesn't miss all the hockey games this season, although he hasn't chosen to go to one in a long time. She talked to his friend recently and set it up so that he would go. And when Jake came home that night after the game, she was waiting for him in bed, happy. And I bet you can guess what they did then.

Now when Lydia looks in Jake's mirror, she sees his love for her that makes her feel beautiful, desired, and taken care of. And, it turns out, it isn't so hard to remember to push that mirror back into place after all.

About the Author

Dr. Jane Greer is a nationally known marriage and family therapist who has been in private practice for over twenty years. She is the author of *How Could You Do This to Me? Learning to Trust after Betrayal*, published by Doubleday; *The Afterlife Connection: A Therapist Reveals How to Communicate with Departed Loved Ones*, by Saint Martin's Press; *Gridlock: Finding the Courage to Move On in Love, Work and Life*; and *Adult Sibling Rivalry*, published in hardcover by Crown and paperback by Fawcett.

She is a contributing editor for *Redbook* magazine and also wrote the "Let's Talk about Sex" advice column for *Redbook* magazine online. She has appeared as a regular guest expert on numerous national television programs, among them *Oprah*, the *Today* show, the *Early Show*, *Dateline*, CNN News, CBS News, *The View*, *20/20*, and *Anderson Cooper 360°*. She also has been interviewed repeatedly for articles in many well-respected publications, including the *New York Times*, *New York Post*, *New York*

Newsday, People magazine, *US, In Touch, Redbook, Ladies' Home Journal,* and *Cosmopolitan.*

She is the host of her own weekly radio Internet show, *Doctor On Call,* which covers health, psychology, beauty, and a broad range of topics that touch us all. *Doctor On Call* is a live hour-long show at www.healthylife.net, every Tuesday at 2 PM Eastern time, 11 AM Pacific time. Her diverse and exciting guests have included comedian Joan Rivers, psychic John Edward, and Dr. Nancy Snyderman.

Every last Tuesday of the month, *Doctor On Call,* www.healthy life.net, features the *Let's Talk Sex* show. Listeners can call in at 800-555-5453 or 310-371-5444 and ask Dr. Greer anything and everything they want to know about sex.

Dr. Greer is a broadcast commentator for featured news stories on her "Heroes and Happy Living" segment, which you can tune into every Monday at www.healthylife.net News@7.